She's One in a Million

When Trusting God Isn't Easy

Janet Zimmermann

Scripture quotations taken from the New American Standard Bible® (NASB),

Copyright © 1960, 1962, 1963, 1968, 1971, 1972, 1973,

1975, 1977, 1995 by The Lockman Foundation

Used by permission: Lockman.org

Certain stock imagery © BigStock Images

Any people depicted in stock imagery provided by BigStock are models, and such images are being used for illustrative purposes only.

Formatting by Daniel J. Mawhinney
40daypublishing.com

Cover design by Jonna Feavel
40daygraphics.com

Author Photo by Richard Weimer

Printed in the United States of America

CONTENTS

DEDICATION

The words you will read in this book may at times bring you to tears, as they have for me. The words you will read will also challenge you to continue to believe for the impossible, as they have for me. The words you will read will also inspire you, as they have for me, and that inspiration comes from Emily herself.

Emily has walked through her journey with grace, strength and dignity. She has always thought of others instead of herself. When we would be facing another surgery, she would be worried about those of us waiting for her, saying that at least she would be asleep. When I would say, "I wish I could take your place," her reply would be, "I'm glad you don't have to."

She never has a pain-free day. She has tried more prescriptions and alternative medicine options than I can count. She builds relationships with her doctors and pharmacists because she sees them so often, but she rarely complains.

Emily shares her story not to garner sympathy, but to encourage and give hope to those in desperate and difficult situations. My favorite response to one of her public presentations came from a high school girl. Through tears, she told Emily, "I have had thoughts of suicide recently, but after hearing your story, I know I can work through this and come out better on the other side."

Emily, you are my hero and I am your biggest fan. This book is for you. I love you.

ACKNOWLEDGMENTS

First and foremost, I am so thankful that my Heavenly Father held me during the most difficult time of my life and continues to hold and guide me. I truly give Him all the glory, honor and praise.

I am thankful for my husband, John. This book is the story from my perspective, but he also experienced the pain of watching a child endure such a difficult experience. Together we are cheering Emily on in life, and I am so grateful that he signed on to be her "Human Guide Dog" for her college career.

Thank you Andrew, Matthew, and Sarah. Life was put on hold for a few years when all the attention was directed toward your sister and her health. You have each been so caring and loving toward Emily and at different times have said exactly what she needed to hear.

Thank you Lisa Dixon. You encouraged me to journal through that time, and then you encouraged me to put it all into a book. You told me the process wouldn't be easy (and you were so right!), but I know that it will be worth it. I will never forget the things you did and the words you said to me during that horrible time.

Thank you Mary Thomas for being there for me after it was "over." The best part is that you were and continue to be there for Emily. The miles we walked and jogged, the mountains we have climbed and the trips we have taken, have all been such a treasure, joy, and delight.

Thank you to my copy editor, Kirk Woundy. What I thought was "Plan B" was the best thing that could have happened. From your first response to my request, I knew you were the right person for this very important task.

Finally, thank you to the Ridgeway Church community for believing in me and my story, and for offering your financial support to make this happen. The weekend Emily and I spent with you was so special, and our friendships with each of you hold a very special place in our hearts.

Note to the Reader

My journal provides the backbone of this book, and most entries are shared exactly as I wrote them each day. As I turned the journal into a manuscript, though, I did occasionally add a parenthetical "note" to provide hindsight and add context to certain entries.

PROLOGUE

December 7, 1941, the day Pearl Harbor was attacked, has long been known as a day of infamy in our country. December 7, 2007 is a day of infamy in my family. That is the day we were attacked.

My husband, John, is a pastor. We had been lifelong residents of Minnesota when John accepted a call to pastor a church in a small South Carolina town in 1996. We have four children: Andrew, Matthew, Emily, and Sarah. This story is about Emily, our third-born, who was 14 years old in December 2007.

I had never taken the good health of my family for granted. I regularly thanked God for that blessing. We had gone several years without good health insurance, and the Lord had been so faithful during that time. In 10 years, we had gone to the doctor once for a sick visit. I saw this as part of the principle of sowing and reaping. We had been sowing good seed into the kingdom, and we were reaping a harvest of good health.

In 2006, after having worked part-time as a sales associate at a retail store at our local mall, I became an assistant manager. The new position provided me with excellent health insurance and other benefits that would prove monumental.

I homeschooled each of my children until the ninth grade; after that, they attended a public high school. A close friend from my church taught at this particular school, and because it was a smaller school with good discipline, I felt it was a good place to enroll them. One of my sons graduated in May 2007; my second son would graduate the following year. In between, Emily started her freshman year, in August 2007.

Emily made the transition from homeschool to public school quite well. She formed good friendships, loved her teachers, and was making good grades. But she started to complain about headaches in October. She would say, "My headache is the size of Japan."

I have had chronic headaches for years and was treated by a chiropractor regularly, which kept them controlled. I just assumed Emily was experiencing a genetic "curse." So I talked to my chiropractor about Emily, and she was happy to try to help.

Around that same time, Emily started having difficulty seeing the board at school. My husband has had glasses since he was a child, so naturally I thought glasses would correct her sight. I made an appointment to see an optometrist.

Emily also seemed more tired than a typical 14-year-old. I attributed that to her getting used to a high school schedule after having been homeschooled for so long.

I took her for the eye appointment, and halfway through the exam, the whistling older optometrist stopped whistling. He said he had to get his assistant to do another test. After that test was done, he came out to tell me that the vision was so bad in her left eye that he couldn't correct it with lenses. She actually couldn't see the big "E" on the eye chart when her right eye was covered. Saying he thought it was a vascular problem, he arranged for us to see a retina specialist.

Two appointments later, the specialist still couldn't figure out why Emily couldn't see much out of her left eye. (Her right eye was only slightly affected.)

The day was December 7, 2007. I took Emily to a third appointment with the specialist around 3:30 p.m., prepared to tell him that we wanted an MRI. Although we had requested this procedure before, he hadn't felt it was warranted. At the end of this appointment, he said, "I'll order an MRI, but I don't think we'll find anything."

There was an MRI machine downstairs from his office, and he called down at 4:45 p.m. to see if Emily could be tested that day. They must have said yes rather reluctantly, because we were rushed from one office to the other. Everything was happening so quickly, and I couldn't help but feel anxious as we proceeded with this critical test. Though still sure that it wasn't a big deal, I wanted to know what was wrong.

We arrived to hear the office workers talking on the phone saying they would be late getting home because they had just gotten another patient. They made calls to my insurance company to make sure it would cover the cost and to see which radiologist was in my plan. Then they added that it might be too late in the day for a radiologist to read the MRI, and that we may have to wait until Monday for the results.

Just then, the specialist from upstairs came down on his way out to make sure everything was going okay. He told them that they needed to have the MRI read that evening, then told me that he would call us with the results that night.

The MRI finally started at about 6 p.m. Because Emily had never been in an MRI machine before and was afraid, I was able to stay in the room with her. I tried to pray, but I was becoming anxious about everything, was tired from the long day and the stress of it all, and just couldn't gather my thoughts together. I saw my teenage daughter in this enormous machine, with loud noises ringing, beeping, and thumping. We had not been warmly received by the office, and I could only imagine how scared she was by this whole ordeal.

At the midway point, the technician stopped to inject the contrast into Emily's arm. Emily has very small veins, and after attempting three times and still not hitting a vein, the nurse said she didn't want to try again. She said we could come back Monday and start from this point in the process. My maternal instincts kicked in and I pushed a little bit, inquiring if there were any other options for us because we lived 45 minutes away and we needed the test and the results immediately. She mentioned that they had a pediatric nurse on staff who had just left; she was willing to call her to see if she could come back.

She was able to reach the nurse, who graciously said she would return and administer the contrast. It took another 30 minutes, but this nurse got it on the first try, and they were able to proceed with the MRI. (Note: Looking back, I feel that the technician must have seen something in the film, because she treated us so much better during the break than she had at the beginning, when she seemed not too thrilled about taking another patient.)

It was about 8 p.m. when we left, and both of us were tired and hungry. I had to make a stop at a Christian bookstore to pick up a song called "All is Well," which I wanted to sing at our Christmas Eve service, just a few weeks away. We also picked up something to eat and began the drive home.

About halfway there, my cell phone rang with a call from John. He said, "The doctor called, and Emily has a brain tumor."

My heart stopped at the enormity of his words. There had to be a mistake. But John kept on repeating back to me what the eye specialist had said. There was a top pediatric neurologist nearby with whom he would schedule a visit. The specialist would make an appointment for us on Monday and would call us with the details. Both he and the radiologist felt that the initial diagnosis was a benign tumor called a craniopharyngioma. This early diagnosis was made based on the location of the tumor, the size, and Emily's age.

There is really no way to describe the emotions I felt at that moment. How would I tell my daughter that she has a brain tumor? I was in shock. I was numb.

Emily asked me what the doctor said. I told her that there was a growth that would have to be removed. We were both silent, absorbed in our own thoughts for the rest of the way home.

We arrived home to John and my son Matthew, both with tear-filled eyes. Emily fell into her Daddy's arms, while Matthew and I clung to one another and cried. John and Matthew had been reading online information about the tumor (not always a good thing?!); when they relayed it, that put a good dose of fear in me.

A bit later, Emily and Matthew went to their rooms, pretty much knowing that sleep wouldn't come. John went to his office and I went to my bedroom. He told me several days later that he had written a poem during the time in his office (1). I sobbed until I couldn't cry anymore. I tried to pray, but I had never felt like God was so far away. The Word says, "I will never leave you or forsake you" (Joshua 1:5). I felt forsaken at that moment. I hoped that somehow I would wake up in the morning only to realize that this had been a horrible nightmare.

CHAPTER 1

December 8 ... Today I hosted the Annual Christmas Tea for the ladies in my church. I prepared the food and went through all the motions, numbed by the pain of what I am going through but not yet ready to share that pain with anyone. Once I got home, family and friends had begun finding out and all were offering their support, love, and prayers.

My mother-in-law is a prayer warrior and a woman of God. She had been reading her Bible when John called her and told her what was happening. She listened, cried, and asked questions. She went back to reading her Bible and was reading in Ephesians about "fainting not in tribulation" (Ephesians 3:13). That concept was beyond any natural comprehension.

I have begun asking God, "Why?" I know that God can handle my questions, I just don't know if I will get any answers.

Emily's spirit is sweet and compassionate. She has an aunt, uncle, and cousins who aren't believers. She said, "If I have to go through this, I'm going to believe for their salvation." There is also a man in our church who has been diagnosed with a neurological condition similar to ALS. She has added her faith to the church family in believing for a supernatural healing for a disease with no cure.

Our music minister has shared with us that a few weeks ago, he felt like the Lord awakened him in the night. He felt the Lord said to be on guard and to pray because the enemy was looking to attack God's chosen. He said that he and his wife have been praying ever since that night. He told us that he feels the warning has given time to prepare for the battle and to believe for the victory!

December 10 … We had been expecting a call all weekend from the eye specialist with an appointment time with the surgeon on Monday. He hadn't called, so I called him first thing in the morning. He apologized and said the surgeon had been out of town, but he gave us the number of a pediatric neurologist with whom to make an appointment today.

After examining Emily and asking her myriad questions, she gave us the same diagnosis—a craniopharyngioma. She said it is normally benign but will generally affect the pituitary gland and all of its functions. Emily's tumor is pushing on her optic nerve, therefore causing the loss of vision in her left eye.

This neurologist wouldn't answer many of our questions, deferring them to the surgeon. She then gave Emily her medical file and asked her to take it out to the receptionist.

With Emily out of the room, she told us that the tumor is very large and that she doesn't know if the optic nerve is permanently damaged or not. She also said that the surgeon we are scheduled to see is the best and, because of that, is very busy. She said when we see him, we need to push for surgery as soon as possible. I left feeling as if I been punched and gotten the wind knocked out of me.

We had phone calls to make when we got home because everyone wanted the details. We asked them to pray for favor with the surgeon in the scheduling of the surgery.

December 11 … We saw the surgeon today. The reality of what we were facing set in very quickly. The doctor walked in and after shaking our hands said, "Because of the size of this tumor, I have rearranged my schedule and we will operate next Monday." God certainly answered the prayers for a quick operating date!

We then saw the scan and were amazed at the size of the tumor. It takes up all the space in the optic chasm, every little space that it could. The surgeon feels that the vision loss will be irreversible. He said the hospital stay will be at least a week, within the ICU for three to five days of that week. The surgery will take between five to seven hours, and we will get hourly updates. Emily received a prescription for her headaches, as well as steroids to prepare her for the surgery.

We have a family of six. None of my children have ever been in the hospital for anything—and now we are facing brain surgery. He also told us that this tumor has a prevalence of one in a million.

Emily can no longer read because her vision is so blurry. Tonight she asked me to email the uncle she has been praying for. Her email said, "I'm scared but I know Jesus loves me very much and that everything is going to be okay."

My boss at work is also a friend and a Christian. She has said she will work with me as well as she can in regard to my schedule. It's the middle of the busiest time of year for a retail business! I've gone back to work, but it has been tough for me to separate myself from what is happening with Emily. Somehow making credit card goals and selling clothes isn't that important!

Because of the size of our town, word has gotten around fast about what Emily is facing. I'll be in my "zone" at work, focused on the needs of the business, when a well-meaning acquaintance will come to the store to ask about Emily. Most of the time, it takes everything within me to hold myself together.

The first semester at school is ending and exams are about to begin before the winter break. Emily's been in no shape to take them. She's tired and she can't see very well. I have been in touch with the school to see what her options might be. The plan is that a teacher will come out over the weekend and Emily will take her exams before her Monday surgery. (Note: We were fine with this, but it was about to get better!)

December 12 … I received a call from the guidance counselor at school to tell me that Emily's teachers have been given permission to average her grades for the first semester and to use them as her exam grade, thereby exempting her from all the exams! We are thrilled and feel so blessed that God has answered a prayer we hadn't even prayed! It's a boost to my faith that God will be faithful during the surgery.

Last night Emily had trouble sleeping. She was going to read her Bible but was unable to read the small print, so she prayed instead. She woke up in the morning sensing a remarkable peace. The Word declares "a peace which passes all understanding" (Philippians 4:7). She had an amazing calm during this time, and it certainly wasn't anything like I was feeling.

We had one more MRI before the Monday surgery. I certainly believed that God could do a miracle and the tumor be removed. John and I were in the room—wearing hospital-issued earplugs—with Emily as she had this scan. We prayed and I was reminded of the scripture that says, "When the enemy steals, he has to repay the believer seven times" (Proverbs 6:30-31). I counted the six family members she was believing for their salvation, and for the man with ALS symptoms! That totaled up to seven! I was also reminded of John's father, who had passed away in July 2002. He loved all of his grandchildren so much and was a wonderful grandfather. He used to call Emily "the fairest in the land." I had an overwhelming sense that he saw us from his home in heaven and was gathering support on her behalf.

We saw the surgeon for a final visit before the surgery and to discuss the results of the MRI. He came into the room and said, "I couldn't sleep last night because I was thinking about what the safest way to remove Emily's tumor would be." He said, "I have decided to go in through the top of her head, in between the two hemispheres of the brain, where there is a natural separation." The incision will be made where a headband would sit, and he won't shave her head. (Sarah, our youngest daughter, had already offered to shave her head if Emily had to!) They will braid her hair away from the incision before surgery.

He told us of the possible side effects—stroke, seizures, temporary muteness—and said the guaranteed side effect would be short-term memory loss. This is because the surgery will be performed where the short-term memory is "housed." He said it will be temporary, but could take up to a year to return. He said she probably shouldn't plan on returning to school until the following school year. He also said he may not be able to get the entire tumor because of the size, so a second surgery may be needed.

The doctor then turned and looked directly at Emily and said, "You are a brave young lady." She smiled one of her famous smiles and replied, "Thank you." He then said to us, "I have a daughter who is also 14 years old and reminds me a lot of Emily in her attitude and excellence in school. I will take care of your daughter like she was my own."

Many people have questioned whether we should get a second opinion from a doctor outside our area. Because of the rapid decline in her vision, we haven't felt that we could take time to do that. It would also mean being away from our family during hospital stays. And the moment we heard the doctor say those precious words, I knew we were at the right place, and the right surgeon would be performing the operation.

There have also been well-meaning people who have questioned our decision to go ahead with the surgery, believing that God could heal and remove the tumor. We have believed that as well, but have also believed that if He did, it would be evident with a clear MRI. Now we feel that God will guide the surgeon's hands to remove it.

December 13 … Before the Wednesday night classes at church, we followed the example in the Word and asked for the elders of the church to pray over Emily and anoint her with oil. Emily articulated that those praying would agree in faith with her for the salvation of her unsaved family, healing for the man with ALS, and lastly, that she would be home for Christmas! We got home and there was an email from her uncle and a poem that he had written for her. (2)

Chapter 2

December 14 … Emily had some Christmas gifts that she wanted to give her teachers, and wanted to say "good-bye." We drove to the campus early, before the school day began. One by one she saw them, and they each wished her well.

On our way out of the school, the principal stopped us and had two students with him. He said, "These students want to ask your permission to do something." One girl said, "Next Monday morning, the day of Emily's surgery, we would like to have prayer at the flagpole for her." Through my tears, I replied, "Of course, we would be honored to have you do that." As they walked away, the principal asked if we would come into the office. There, a group of about 15 faculty and staff joined hands in a circle and prayed. They each prayed a prayer for Emily, as well as for others. What a blessing!

I got home from work around 11:15 p.m. I went up to check on Emily, and she was wide awake. Between the high doses of steroids she is taking and the stress of her situation, she is struggling with insomnia.

We talked for over an hour. She told me she asked God why this was happening to her. She wondered if she had done something to "deserve" this. I told her absolutely not! I said, "I may not understand any of this, but what I do know is that God is always faithful and He will be with us." I told her that I would take her place if there was a way for me to do so.

I then sobbed myself to sleep, asking the same question of God—"Why Emily?"

A dear friend from Minnesota has a daughter who is a surgical nurse for a top neurosurgeon in Minneapolis. She also used to be Emily's favorite babysitter when we lived in Minnesota. I have been in touch with her and she has been a good listener for me, often explaining details that sound like medical jargon. I asked her, "Could you talk to the surgeon you work for and ask him about this case, as well as about our surgeon?" She was happy to do so and came back to me with one phrase from him: "He is a good man." That means that he knows of our surgeon, and has researched him and his credentials. He also said, after seeing a copy of our MRI, that the way our surgeon plans to operate is the best option available. It is another confirmation—a second opinion—that we are at the right place.

December 15 … Saturday nights are unusual in a pastor's home. Our tradition is that I make homemade pizza. John usually will go to church to study there, and did so tonight. This night was different from all others in the past, and we know things will be different from now on.

The lights on the Christmas tree were on, and the kids and I were all sitting around it in the family room. We shared special holiday memories and laughed and had a special time together. The day had been busy with family and friends calling and stopping by. Emily finally said, "I'm so glad that tonight is just my family. I'm happy for all the people that have come by, but now I am ready to go to bed."

CHAPTER 3

December 17 … .The day arrived, and I wish I could say I was prepared for it. It would have been nice to sleep in, but the steroids kept Emily from sleeping, and I had too much on my mind for sleep to come. Emily and I finished packing our bags for the hospital. I had planned ahead for food at home for the family to eat, depending on who might happen to be home. I didn't know what to expect.

We were at the hospital by 11:30 a.m. for the noon start. We were called, and after Emily changed into the hospital gown, our whole family went back into the prep room. The staff commented on how many of us were in there! The nurses checked her vitals, and we had to sign a release that stated that we knew what the risks of the surgery were. We also had to sign a permission form allowing Emily to be anesthetized.

All this time, Emily was so brave; yes, she was nervous, but she was handling what was before her with a maturity far beyond her years. I was allowed to put on scrubs and walk beside her as she was wheeled to the operating room. The anesthetist was telling jokes on the way, with the nurses chiming in, to keep the mood light.

Nothing could have prepared me for walking into the room where brain surgery would be performed on my daughter. The doors swung open and I felt the full magnitude of it all. Emily was moved onto the operating table and was asked what flavor gas she wanted to go to sleep with; she chose bubble gum. They explained to her what was going to happen and put the mask on her face. I whispered, "I love you, Sweetie, and I'll be there when you wake up."

In 30 seconds, she was out. She looked so small in that big room full of equipment that would be used on her for the next four to six hours.

The nurse walked me out to the waiting room. I had been so strong up to now for Emily's sake, but on that walk, I started falling apart. The nurse said, "We'll take good care of her, she'll be fine." I stepped into the waiting room and started sobbing. I felt an incredible sense of helplessness. There was absolutely nothing I could do for her. She was in the Lord's hands. Many prayers had gone up for the Lord's presence to permeate that operating room, for the Lord's hand to guide the surgeon's and give him wisdom, and for guardian angels to watch and keep Emily safe in the hands of God.

We received the first call 45 minutes later: She was doing fine, and the surgery was about to begin. I had brought scripture verses to pray, my Bible, books, etc., to help make the time pass more quickly. It was extremely difficult to concentrate on anything other than the fact that my daughter was having brain surgery. We continued to get hourly updates and each one was similar: "Emily is doing fine."

Matthew talked to one of his friends from school while we were waiting. I asked him about the prayer for Emily that morning. By South Carolina standards, it had been a cold morning—31 degrees! But around the flagpole that morning, nearly 30 students and staff had prayed for a successful surgery. We were so blessed by this outpouring of support for her.

After four hours, the call came that they would be done in the next two hours. Finally, after almost six hours, the surgeon came out and shook our hands and, with a smile on his face, said, "Everything went well. I feel like I got it all, but we will have an MRI in the morning to not only see if we got it all, but to make sure there is no swelling." He then hugged both John and me. I have had very little experience with pediatric neurosurgeons (okay, none), but I don't think they usually hug the patient's parents!

We went down to the Pediatric Intensive Care Unit, and were called in as she was beginning to stir. She never looked so beautiful! We had been told that she could still have a breathing tube or a drainage tube, but she had neither. She also had no bandages, and the incision site looked good.

While waiting for her to wake up, I came out so Sarah could go in to see her. While she was in there, Emily, with her eyes still shut, signed M-O-M to Sarah with sign language! Sarah came out and I went back in. Emily woke up and talked a little. The family took turns going in until around 10 p.m., when they all left to go home.

It wasn't very long until she needed pain medicine for the headache. It didn't seem to help much, because she started crying and through her tears cried out, "I hate this. It is torture and traumatic." I held her and tried to reassure her that it was going to get better.

A short time later, in a matter-of-fact tone, she said, "Hospitals aren't all they're cracked up to be." Where that came from, I have no idea! (Note: This was the first of many nights we would have listening to machines beeping and ringing, babies crying in another room, and nurses coming in every hour.)

CHAPTER 4

December 18 … The surgeon's nurse came in to check on Emily in the morning. She reiterated that Emily would have an MRI sometime during the day. Emily was thrilled to be able to eat breakfast. I did find out real soon just how "short" her short-term memory is. She couldn't remember what she ate five minutes after she finished eating! We tried to make light of this lapse in her memory, because she is used to having a really good one.

Matthew came up later in the morning and was eating almond trail mix. Emily doesn't like almonds, and when Matthew asked, "Emily, do you like almonds? Do you think you used to?" she replied, "Matthew, do you think I'm stupid?!" She remembers pretty much everything up until coming to the hospital—including her likes and dislikes!

The surgeon came in to see her late in the afternoon with news I didn't want to hear. On the MRI, he saw a small spot close to the carotid artery, which had been impossible for him to see while performing the surgery. He said it could be a piece of tumor, but it could also be a cyst that would go away on its own. We saw the before and after scans and couldn't believe the difference and how large the tumor was. He said it had been 3 inches around—the size of a baseball.

The moment he left, I made a decision to believe that God could "take care" of the spot, no matter what type of tissue it was. He had proved His faithfulness through a dangerous surgery. A few days ago, the scripture I had read from Psalms was, "I will live and not die and declare the works of the Lord" (Psalms 118:17). I feel like the Lord has impressed on me that Emily's sickness was not unto death.

One other side effect the surgeon mentioned was that Emily's body may have difficulty maintaining its proper fluid levels because of where the surgery was performed; he doesn't know the extent of damage to the pituitary gland. The pituitary gland secretes a hormone that causes stability to the fluid in the body.

Twenty-four hours after surgery, Emily wasn't keeping any fluids in. She received some medication to help, but as was predicted, the pendulum swung the other way and then she wasn't able to get rid of the fluids. We were told this is called "DI," or diabetes insipidus. With DI, excessive thirst leads to excretion of large amounts of severely dilute urine, and no reduction of fluid intake affects the concentration of the urine. (Note: Of course we had never heard of this before, and had no idea what the effects of it would be.)

Chapter 5

December 19 ... The ICU is a great place to receive excellent care, but not a good place to sleep! The nurses come in every hour to take vital signs. Emily had a catheter/foley, and the doctors wanted to monitor how much urine she was putting out in order to administer the correct doses of medication to counteract the DI. But because of her memory issues, Emily would forget that she had it; I would wake up to see her try to get out of bed to go to the bathroom. I would tell her that it was okay, she didn't have to worry about it, but she couldn't get her mind around the fact that she wasn't going to wet the bed, and it really bothered her.

Her headaches have finally lessened, and she is receiving very little pain medication. Our surgeon stopped by, but just to see how she was doing and to tell us he was leaving to go on vacation until after Christmas.

Because the hospital is a "teaching" hospital, there are usually six to 10 doctors doing rounds with the staff doctor each morning. In addition to the neurology staff, Emily is being seen by a team of endocrinologists. Emily really needs to see a pediatric endocrinologist, but the one who was at the hospital recently left and only comes back one day a week. Because everything Emily is dealing with is so unusual and pediatric-specific, the endocrinologists who treat adults have tried to hold off answering most of the questions we've asked. I feel like there are so many doctors involved and not one main doctor keeping everyone on the same page.

Emily had the same nurse again, and she was fantastic. Emily has been so hot since the surgery. The nurses lowered the thermostat (I had a sweatshirt on and a blanket around me), and she was still hot. I fanned her until my arms got tired. Finally, the nurse said, "I'm going to find her a fan." She came back a few minutes later with one. She put it on the end of her bed and Emily was thrilled!

I had to go back to work for the first time since her surgery, so John came and plans to stay until I can come back. It was very hard for me to leave. In the two days that I have been with her, we have gotten into a routine. I always check with the nurse to make sure the meds they are giving her are correct, and I can sense when she needs something. I've been patient with her asking me the same questions 10 times—literally! She would say, "What time do you work tomorrow?" I would answer, and within a minute, she would ask me the same thing again.

Once home, I went through mail and telephone messages. There were endless calls to make to family and friends who wanted updates. As much as I know they want to know all the details, it has been so difficult telling the same story—sometimes five or six times in a row.

Our music minister's wife left a message that she had a meal for us, so I called her and she stopped by. What she told me during her visit hit me hard. She said that before school started, Emily had asked her to pray with her. Emily asked for her to agree with her in prayer for the salvation of her aunt and uncle. She also asked that as she was starting high school, that God would use her mightily for Him!

Do I think it is fair that God is using Emily in this way? Absolutely not! But I have to believe that God is going to use the hell that we are walking through to glorify Him.

December 20 … It was so nice to sleep in my own bed! It was so quiet and peaceful at home. Nevertheless, Emily is never far from my mind. I called John as soon as I woke up in the morning. Boy, did he have a story to tell!

During the night, he said, he had dozed off and was awakened to alarms going off, the lights being turned on, and a swarm of staff rushing into the room. He woke up to see blood everywhere! He asked what happened. The nurse said, "She pulled her IV out of her arterial vein." Her special blanket, "Mimi," was covered in blood and was about to be thrown out, but John told them they'd better not.

It took them three attempts to get another vein. Finally they did, but after a short time, she pulled it out again. This time, she re-wrapped all the tape around her hand and laid the IV neatly on top! They didn't try again.

Because of her memory issues, she didn't remember doing it at all. She has complained that it bothered her, but I guess none of us realized how much, and the extent to which she would go to take care of it! I told John to soak the blanket in water in the sink and I would bring it home and wash it when I came later in the day. (Note: It did survive!)

I worked a 10-to-6 shift at work, came home and picked up a meal that had been left for our family, and went back up to the hospital. Emily ate a little, but not much appeals to her. She has said some pretty funny things. John said, "I am going stir crazy and I don't know if I can make it another day," to which Emily replied with a straight face, "I can't believe you're saying that about me—that you don't want to stay with me." She looked as if she was about to cry. Of course John felt horrible, and then she started laughing!

The night nurses came in to check on her and asked her not to repeat the antics from the night before. She had heard about it enough that even though she didn't remember doing it, she knew what had happened. She looked at them so seriously and said, "I'm sorry." It was hard leaving again, but I have to be at work at 8 tomorrow morning.

CHAPTER 6

December 21 … It was an 8-to-5 day for me at work, and it ended up being a really tough day. I have honestly tried my best to separate personal from work, but I have had my moments. Today I was told that everyone has "stuff" that they are dealing with—to me, the insinuation was that mine is no different or more difficult than anyone else's—and that basically life sucks sometimes so I just need to get over it. I was told that I need to step it up at work.

There is a scripture that talks about a standard of protection surrounding God's children (Jeremiah 51:12). I feel like I am being swallowed up and am having a hard time staying afloat, and where is that standard when I need it? I survived the day, went home to pick up food that a friend had made, and left for the hospital. John ate and then left for home, as I am to stay the night.

A nurse we haven't had before came in and asked if Emily's hair had been washed yet. When we said that it hadn't, she checked on her other patients and came back with everything we needed to do it.

Sarah and I began by taking out the braids that held back her hair from the incision. They were caked with blood, and with the medicine used to clean the wound. The strands of hair were so stiff that they were very hard to take out! I couldn't believe how many times we had to rinse her hair before the water wasn't red. After the hair wash and a sponge bath, she put on her own pajamas for the first time. She was exhausted, but felt so much better.

I talked with John on the phone, and he told me that earlier in the day, Emily asked about Grandpa (John's father). John reminded her that he had died. She started crying and asked how Grandma was doing. John reminded her that he had died five years earlier. She cried even harder and was so broken about his death again and that she hadn't remembered it.

As John relayed the story to me, I couldn't help but think back to the day of the MRI before the surgery, when I had felt Grandpa's presence so strong. I will always wonder if she felt his presence during the hours of the surgery so strongly that it was like he was alive.

December 22 … We were told this morning by the doctor doing rounds that Emily should be able to leave the ICU today. To us that means the next step before we can go home, and Christmas Eve is two days away. A dear friend and prayer warrior from Colorado called to pray with me over the phone. It was a sweet and tender prayer. We also got the results from pathology back, and the tumor was in fact benign! Even though that is what was expected, it was a praise report to get the facts!

Emily has become a favorite patient to many of the nurses. Her favorite nurse was the one to discharge us to the regular floor. She was sad to see Emily go, but happy that her health was improving enough to move up. Once upstairs, the two of us actually went for a short walk in her new surroundings I had to go to work and close, so Matthew was going to stay the night with her, as John has to preach in the morning.

December 23 … I got up early and did some laundry before leaving for the hospital. The doctors told me that if Emily's sodium levels (caused by the fluid shifts) were stable all day today and during the first part of tomorrow, she could be discharged Christmas Eve!

Matthew stayed again today as I had to work. We closed early on Sunday, so I had time to do some last-minute Christmas shopping, and then came home to wrap gifts, clean the house, do laundry, and return endless phone calls from people who wanted updates. I have to be back at my store by 7 a.m. tomorrow for Christmas Eve shoppers!

CHAPTER 7

December 24 ... Too many people leave their Christmas shopping until the last minute! We were busy—so busy that we ran out of gift cards!

I was still hopeful that Emily would be able to be discharged today. On my break I called to the hospital to check on her numbers. Her sodium levels had been fine at the first blood draw of the morning, and the doctors were still saying that if the afternoon numbers were okay, she could go home.

I was able to leave work at 1 p.m. I stopped to get all of Emily's prescriptions filled, since things were closing early today and would be closed tomorrow, and when I arrived at the hospital, the nurse was beginning the discharge paperwork. Emily's prayer had been answered—she was going to be home for Christmas!

The drive home was tough for Emily in that slight car movements caused her head to hurt, and she was a bit nauseous. We arrived home and she assumed a position on the couch downstairs. (Note: She would maintain this position for many months to come.)

Our church has a special Christmas Eve service every year. I had been planning to sing "All is Well," the song that I had purchased the track for the night we found out about the tumor. Now that song, even though I am not singing it, is a sort of declaration of my faith. All was well in Bethlehem the night Jesus was born. God had promised redemption to His children and because He is the same yesterday, today and forever, I know He is with me through the ordeal we are going through.

Our Christmas Eve tradition is to have a variety of hors d'oeuvres and snacks. I haven't been able to prepare anything because when I'm not working, I am at the hospital. My dear sister-in-law brought over a box of food for me to fix for tonight and also for a big breakfast Christmas morning, things I usually have and also special things that she had fixed. My heart is overwhelmed by her gesture of love for our family.

While we waited for the rest of the family to get home, Emily rested on the couch and cried because the headache was so bad. I gave her pain medication and prayed that it would subside. By the time everyone got home and we started eating, the pain had let up a bit. Emily kept repeating, "I just love Christmas and all the special food!"

We ate and opened gifts. Because of her memory issues, Emily would open a gift, set it down on the coffee table, and five minutes later ask, "Now who did I get that from?" She would ask, "Is that mine?" We began to joke with her that she got to experience Christmas over and over because she didn't remember from whom she had received gifts. She had done all her shopping early and remembered what she had bought for the family.

Tired after all the excitement, Emily went to bed early. My girls used to share a bedroom with twin beds, so John and I have decided that we will take turns sleeping in her room. I wanted to be there tonight, and as I put my head on the pillow, my thoughts will be somewhat bittersweet. I am so happy that she is home, but it is so difficult to see her struggle with her memory. She has always been the child who would remind me of things when I would say, "Don't let me forget … "

My tears today are a mix of thanksgiving—that, hopefully, the ordeal is behind us at least for a while—and also an overwhelming sense of the magnitude of this. Is it over, or is it just beginning?

CHAPTER 8

December 25 … Christmas Day! Emily slept through the night, except for a couple of times when she had to use the bathroom. I gave her a pain pill at 7:15 a.m., and she proceeded to throw up at 9. Memo to self: "Pain pills cannot be taken on an empty stomach." This is our first time dealing with all of this, and I would have thought the pharmacist would have shared that piece of information with me.

I made a big breakfast around 10 and then everyone left to do their own thing, so there was a quiet house for a while. Emily rested and I cleaned up a bit. I have been home so little in the last week that it was just good to be there. Laundry and cleaning don't take holiday breaks!

I helped Emily bathe. Because this was only the second time washing her hair since surgery, the water was still pretty red when rinsing. She was exhausted when we finished and took a nap. She was also in a considerable amount of pain.

I feel so helpless. It isn't like this is a routine illness. Emily has just had brain surgery and, for the most part, I have no idea what to expect. She has been so brave and really has complained very little. We aren't talking about just a regular headache; she certainly has reason to have one mother of all headaches!

December 26 ... I had to work later in the day, so I had a busy morning before I left. In the past, Emily saw a pediatrician once for a minor issue, but she has always been healthy. Because the hospital where we have been going is 45 minutes away, we need a doctor here to know what is going on.

I have some questions about our new doctor being able to understand the complexity of Emily's situation because she is just out of residency. (Note: She would prove to be invaluable over the next several months in her concern for Emily and interaction with the doctors at the hospital. I am so thankful that we didn't switch doctors. She always answered our questions, or found the answer.) She drew blood for lab tests, specifically Emily's sodium levels. It was late in the day, so we haven't gotten the results yet.

December 27 ... Emily went to the bathroom a lot during the night, which was cause for concern. The pediatrician called with the lab results, and her sodium has dropped 10 points in two days. Because of the severity of the headaches, the neurosurgeon ordered a CT scan.

John took her to the hospital because I had to work in the afternoon. By the time John got her to the hospital, Emily was very weak and tired. They did more blood work and wanted to admit her. John got her something to eat while waiting for the results of the scan and labs. We called people to pray that she would stabilize.

The results came back and the sodium levels had come up—just barely, but enough that she could go home! The CT scan didn't show anything that would account for the headaches. She came home and, although tired, felt good enough to play a game of Scrabble with her Grandma!

December 28 ... I was off work today, so I walked and cleaned the house before taking Emily to get lab work. When we got home, she lay down and rested. We had lunch and then I had to go to the store. Matthew was going with me, and Emily said she wanted to try to go. She was tired from the walk into the store, but held on to the cart. We didn't stay long because it really wore her out.

She came home and lay on the couch. I sat beside her and then she said that she felt "weird all over" and felt like she had to throw up. I helped her toward the bathroom, but we didn't make it. She collapsed into a chair that I pushed out with my foot. She didn't completely pass out, because she never lost consciousness, but her head kind of fell back and she was having a difficult time speaking to us.

I called the pediatrician, who thought maybe she had gotten up too fast. It is amazing to me how fast my heart was racing and how scared I was in that moment, yet I could be as calm and rational on the outside for Emily's sake—and also for my other kids, who were pretty freaked out!

A dear friend from Wisconsin called this afternoon to tell us how concerned she and her family are over Emily and how much they love her. She wanted me to know if I ever need to talk or want someone to pray with, that she is available. It means so much knowing that her family, along with so many others, is praying for Emily and our family.

Matthew gave me a letter that Emily had written to us before she went to the hospital. She had written one to each of her siblings as well. I wept as I read, "I love you both so much. You are both being so strong through this and I know it is hard for you, but you are being that way for my sake." I am continually amazed at the maturity she is demonstrating through this. She is only 14½ years old!

December 29 … Emily went to the bathroom a lot during the night again. We have already begun to realize that that is an indication that her sodium levels are shifting. Her pituitary gland isn't able to maintain the fluid levels in her body, so she has a medication that should help her stabilize this. Figuring out the levels isn't an exact science; the doctors don't know if her pituitary gland is producing any of the hormone that regulates her fluid levels, or if medication needs to do all the work. Endocrinologists seem to be guessing in figuring out the exact amount she needs.

I helped Emily write some thank-you notes, and I wrote some for those people who have brought food. We had a storm and our power went out in the house late afternoon. Matthew, Emily, and I went to get a bite to eat, and then Matthew dropped Emily and me off at the door of the grocery store to pick up a few things. We were only in the store for maybe 15 minutes before coming home.

I was walking next to Emily up the stairs into the house when she collapsed again. Matthew carried her in to lay her on the couch. We gave her water to drink and, although weak, she was talking okay. She then went to the bathroom every 15 minutes. I tried calling doctors and either never got through, or was told they didn't know what to do.

When the men all went out for the evening, Emily and I played dominoes and she seemed better. All evening, she kept asking the same questions: "What day is it and what is going on tomorrow?" "When does school start?" "Are there more cookies?!"

December 30 … It was a good day. It almost seems like things are settling in. Emily's headache wasn't as bad, she wasn't as tired, and she didn't collapse at all!

CHAPTER 9

December 31 … I had to work from 9 to 2, so John took Emily to get labs. Afterward, the doctor called me because she couldn't reach John and said Emily needed to go to the hospital immediately. Her sodium levels were too high.

I took her when I got home. The hospital drew more blood, and I was praying that the levels had stabilized and we wouldn't have to stay, but this time we did. We were in the ER for about four hours and then moved up to the regular floor. She kept saying, "I don't want to be here." "I just want things to be normal." "I'm so sick of all of this!"

The doctors needed to get accurate urine levels and wanted to put in a foley again. Her memory isn't very good, but she knows what that is and doesn't want it!

In the quiet and stillness of a hospital room, Emily and I watched the ball drop in Times Square and prayed in the New Year together. After Emily fell asleep, I couldn't help but think the same thoughts she had voiced earlier: When will this end? When will life get back to so some kind of normal? I also thought that the worst year of my life was officially over!

January 1, 2008 … Happy New Year! We didn't get any sleep because the monitors kept beeping all night. The labs in the morning revealed that Emily's sodium levels hadn't gone up anymore, but also hadn't come down at all.

Emily had it in her head that she wanted to take a shower. I told her we needed to ask the nurse because she was still hooked up to a monitor. Just a few minutes later, she asked again and started pulling the monitor behind her to the bathroom. It was a funny sight, and I started laughing. She looked at me so seriously and said, "Well, how would you feel if you wanted to take a shower and couldn't?"

A group of five doctors came in shortly after our conversation. They were asking us a lot of questions as well as reviewing her labs and determining a course of treatment. There was a pause as they were ending their discussion, and Emily said, "Can I ask a question?" Of course they said yes, thinking this would be a great way to share their knowledge with their young patient. She then asked, "Can I please be unplugged from the monitor so I can take a shower?" They replied that she could, but the look of anticipation on their faces while they waited for the big question was priceless!

January 2 … I worked 8 to 5 and then left for the hospital. I can tell the stress of all of this is affecting the whole family. The kids have been bickering among themselves, and that is pretty unusual.

John left the hospital while I was on the way, and Matthew and Sarah came over for a while. We all played a card game with Emily. Her sodium levels have come down a little, but no one has talked about her leaving quite yet. Her memory also seems to be improving. She would ask the same questions, but when I told her the same answer, she'd remember being told.

She is still hot all the time, and I am freezing when I am in the room. She is continually bothered by the foley and keeps asking when it can be taken out.

January 3 … She continued to improve today and her favorite resident doctor came in and said we could go home! She was thrilled to be with "just the family," she said.

After we ate, I went to get her prescriptions filled. John left when I got home to go to the gym, and Emily decided she'd like to take a whirlpool bath in my tub. She didn't stay in too long because she was tired.

She was standing next to the tub drying off when she said she didn't feel well. She sat down on the edge of the tub and "semi" passed out. Her eyes were open, but she couldn't respond when I asked her questions. I yelled for Sarah and Matthew to come and bring the phone. I called John to come home and called a neighbor who is a nurse. After maybe a minute that seemed like an hour, there was no improvement, so I called 9-1-1. I was just finishing giving them the information when she started coming to. The dispatcher said they could still come, and I said I thought we would be okay.

No sooner had I hung up the phone than it happened again. Her breathing was labored this time, and she again couldn't speak and was turning pale. I called the dispatcher back and asked for responders to come. It took the EMTs 20 minutes to get to our house, and by that time John and the neighbor were there and Emily was responsive again. As the ambulance arrived, so did another neighbor, who is a public safety officer. We had a full house!

The EMTs gave her oxygen, checked her vitals, and recommended we take her to the hospital. We called the doctor and explained everything and he said it was our call to make. We decided to stay home.

Again, I can't believe I was able to stay calm during the whole ordeal. I wanted to sit down and sob, but I had to stay calm for Emily and the other kids.

Because she was better when the EMTs arrived, the thought was that her blood pressure had probably dropped as a result of her being in the hot bathtub water after just leaving the hospital. Could someone have told me to not give her a bath?

I don't remember ever being as afraid for her life as I was in those moments.

CHAPTER 10

January 4 ... I worked an 8-to-5 shift today, so John took Emily to her first appointment with a pediatric endocrinologist. She has been seeing adult endocrinologists because there isn't a pediatric endocrinologist on staff at the hospital. Those doctors have helped to a degree, but because all of her issues are pediatric in nature, haven't been entirely confident.

This doctor feels her pituitary gland isn't working at all, and never will. He said it is fine because there is medication that can do everything for her. The pituitary gland, in addition to secreting the hormone that regulates fluid levels, tells the thyroid gland to work and regulates growth, among other things. But all the doctor is concerned about are the fluid shifts, which he said are most important to get regulated right now. He said she could have a "breakthrough," which basically means that she would start going to the bathroom and not be able to stop.

I guess this is a one-step-at-time process. None of this comes easy, and it will take some patience in getting everything just right.

January 5 … Today was a day that makes me think that we have turned a corner. Emily didn't have any breakthroughs, as the doctor warned of, and her headache wasn't bad. She was still tired and spent a lot of the day resting. John and I are still taking turns sleeping in Emily's room—it is starting to get old.

January 6 … Everyone went to church except Emily and me. I helped her go through the gifts she had received while in the hospital. I helped her pick up her side of the bedroom. She likes things neat and orderly and hasn't felt well enough to do anything about the stuff lying around. Her hospital bag still needed unpacking, so I did that for her as well.

I had to work at 2 p.m., so Matthew was left in charge. When I got home, Emily said that he was a great baby-sitter! She must have had an appetite, because Matthew told her she had to stop eating! The surgeon had told us that a possible/probable side effect of her kind of tumor is that the hunger and thirst mechanisms don't function. Most patients neither know when to drink nor ever feel full, so they become obese.

At this point in the process, Emily drinks when she's thirsty (or when we make her drink, if we think her sodium levels are high and she has dehydration symptoms). Generally, she eats very little and then feels full.

She remains very sweet and positive about this whole thing. The surgeon also said that the patient's personality could temporarily change. Hmmm, I wonder what that would be like?!

January 7 … Emily had another good day. She worked on some thank-you notes and then helped me with dinner when I got home from work. The church board has been good to let John work from the house when I have to be at work, so that someone can stay with Emily. He's not used to it, though, and gets a little stir crazy.

I have scheduled another MRI to see if the remaining spot of tumor has dissolved. We are believing that it is gone in the Name of Jesus! We used to sing a song in church: "It's done, yes it's done … through the precious Blood of Jesus, the battle is won!"

January 8 … When all this was starting for Emily, I had a toothache and ended up having a root canal and crown. I had to go to the dentist this morning for an impression, and it was miserable. I kept thinking that this isn't anything compared to what Emily had to go through.

There's a scripture in Mark 9:24 where a man cries out to the Lord, "I believe, but help my unbelief." That's how I feel. I want the faith to believe that everything is going to be okay, but I struggle with being able to fully grasp it. Emily was exhausted tonight, even more than usual, and so of course there is cause for concern in my heart.

January 9 … Emily was still lethargic today and still very tired. She also seemed a little confused when asked questions. While I was at work, Matthew said, she started crying because she is so worried about getting so far behind in school. She said she doesn't remember what she learned the first semester and doesn't want to fail the ninth grade. Matthew also doesn't want her to have to repeat the ninth grade.

I should be worrying about her schooling, but I am so much more concerned about the stability of her health right now, that school has been put on the back burner.

January 10 … When I was walking this morning, I personalized this scripture: "No weapon (cyst) formed against us (Emily) will prosper (grow)" (Isaiah 54:17). Emily seemed lethargic and tired today. I called the doctor and he wanted us to go get labs drawn. John took her, as I had to be at work at 1 p.m.

When the results came back, John was told to take her to the ER right away. This time Emily didn't go to the regular floor, but back into the Pediatric ICU. I am weary and tired and I don't understand why this keeps going on like it does. Balancing the pressure at work to stay on top of the numbers and the concern at home about Emily is not getting any easier. It is a multi-front battle—a brain tumor that won't go away, and trips to the ER like they are trips to Target!

January 11 … I didn't sleep at all last night—gee, I wonder why? Work was stressful, and with Emily back in the hospital, I stopped at home to change and left to go up there for the night. Emily's sodium levels did not stabilize at all during the day. They continued to drop. She looked pitiful when I saw her—very tired and weak. She hadn't eaten much all day. They did a CT scan to make sure everything was okay neurologically, and it was. She doesn't have an IV, and they are drawing blood every six hours. Normally she winces when they stick her, but today she kind of just lies there. I am hopeful that things will stabilize overnight.

January 12 … Sometimes there is little sleep in the ICU, and then, at other times, none at all. Last night was one of those times. The stabilizing that I was hoping and praying for didn't happen. She seemed worse this morning. We woke up to find out that Emily had wet the bed during the night. She was absolutely mortified at the thought of that happening. When it happened, I knew things were not right.

A resident came in to check on Emily and I was thinking she might have missed her calling, because being a doctor doesn't suit her! She didn't seem to have any concern or empathy for her patient. She was extremely short with the responses to the questions I was asking.

Emily was sitting up in a chair and I asked her if she wanted to "talk" to Sarah via Instant Messenger on the computer. She started typing, and it wasn't making sense. John called me right away from home because Sarah had shown it to him. He said, "How can she be worse today after being in the hospital for almost two days and the sodium levels have come down?" I would ask Emily a question and she would start a response and then mumble the rest.

The non-helpful resident was outside the room and I took the computer out to show her what was happening. She had no clue, but said she would talk to another doctor, order another CT scan, and increase the steroid stress dose Emily was taking. A neurologist came to examine her and made the determination that it wasn't neurological. They ruled out seizures and strokes. They "thought" it was her body dealing with the sodium imbalances—the ups and downs of it. They said to give it time—easy for them to say.

The boys came by so I could get away from the hospital for a little bit. They couldn't believe how much she had deteriorated since they last saw her, and it really bothered them. She rested most of the afternoon and seemed a tiny bit better in the evening. I helped the nurse bathe her, and she was so sweet to take time to braid Emily's hair so it would stay out of the way.

I am exhausted. Before going to bed, however, I read Psalm 20 to Emily: "May the Lord answer in the day of trouble … may He send help and support … we will sing for joy over victory (Emily's!). May the Lord fulfill your petitions. I know the Lord saves His anointed … He will answer from heaven with the strength of His right hand. We boast in the Name of the Lord. We have risen and stood upright. May the King answer us in the day we call." Amen!

January 13 … Maybe someday I will get sleep again …

Emily wet the bed again, and this morning it was like it didn't even faze her. She was awake, but not alert. She sat up in a chair to eat and had taken a bite or two of her cereal when I noticed she didn't look quite right. I asked her if she was okay, and she said her head hurt really badly. Then she started throwing up and continued for several minutes.

I was trying to get the attention of a nurse to help me and I couldn't. I felt so helpless. Even though I had raised four children, I had never seen an episode like this before. I was scared. It was everywhere in the small room. Finally a nurse came in and helped me. This, of course, weakened Emily even more. She was not speaking clearly at all. She also didn't seem fazed at all by what had just happened.

A doctor came in and I said, "Something isn't right. Can you please figure out what is wrong?" Another neurologist came and examined her again and came to the same conclusion—a fluid imbalance that will take time to stabilize. He said he wanted to wait another day to order an MRI.

Leaving to go to work was the hardest thing I've had to do. Other times when I have left, I've known she would be fine. This time, I didn't have that confidence.

I came back after work, bringing along an incredible deep-fried turkey meal that my neighbor made. (It is such a blessing because cooking isn't high on my "to-do list," and my family still needs to eat.) I walked into Emily's room and, where she would always greet me with, "Hi Mommy," this time she didn't. She looked at me as if she didn't know who I was. The sentence she did speak made no sense at all. I couldn't believe that this child had walked on her own into the hospital just a few days ago and now had lost all control of her body, couldn't speak, and could barely keep her eyes open!

After she fell asleep, John told me that he had a "come to Jesus" talk with the resident with whom I hadn't been impressed. He told her, "My daughter walked into this hospital talking, and now she can hardly move. Something is wrong and if you don't know what's wrong, tell me that, but I want someone to figure it out." An MRI was ordered, but like the CT scan, it didn't show anything abnormal.

Something isn't right, someone is missing something, but it doesn't seem like anyone cares enough to figure it out.

CHAPTER 11

January 14 … I came home late and cried myself to sleep. I was awakened at 1:30 a.m. by a call from John. He said another doctor had come in, and they had a long talk while Emily was sleeping. He felt like she truly listened, and didn't just blow us off.

This doctor felt like Emily could be depressed. John wasn't sure if that was all of it, but he went along with her diagnosis for the time being.

She proceeded to turn on all the lights in the room and told Emily to wake up because she had been sleeping too much. The doctor started asking her all kinds of questions, stimulating her mind. Emily started engaging and even laughing. She spoke to me on the phone and sounded like herself for the first time in three days! John said that Emily told him that it wasn't that she "couldn't" talk, she just didn't want to.

My joy didn't last long, because she started slipping back again this evening. Her speech became labored again. It's almost like she knows something isn't right, but she can't make it right.

Sarah and I tried to cheer her up. Then the PICU staff doctor came in and said that we shouldn't have been given the MRI results without a proper read. Apparently the weekend staff had just said it "looked fine," when in fact there had been a problem. Emily's brain stem has swollen from the fluctuation of the fluid shifts. That is consistent with the physical problems she has been experiencing. He said the worst was probably over and the swelling will diminish. FINALLY, we have answers!

Emily hardly speaks at all, but we played "Phase 10" and she was able to do that. Even though it is still difficult to see Emily like she is, at least we know what it is and that it is temporary.

January 15 ... My night shift wasn't nearly as "exciting" as John's had been. Emily still wasn't talking, but now she seemed uncomfortable. Without warning, she sat up in the bed and vomited everywhere. She still had no control of her bladder and wasn't even aware that she didn't.

In the morning, she had her favorite day nurse, and that seemed to cheer her up. The doctor and residents came by and asked what she was eating. I said, "Not much—there isn't a lot of variety or taste to the hospital food." The doctor agreed and said I should get her whatever she wanted to eat. I made a quick trip to the grocery store and bought her Stouffer's macaroni and cheese (her favorite!) and some Oreos. She ate a little bit of the food, and although her stomach hurt, she kept it down.

The surgeon came by in the late afternoon, having been briefed on how the weekend went. He said the latest MRI still showed a piece of tumor and it wasn't just a cyst, so another surgery would be necessary. He said we could do it as soon as we wanted or we could wait—but with the risk that it could grow and cause further complications.

Having it now will further delay her being able to finish the ninth grade with her classmates, but will also give her finality, as well as a summer vacation. Waiting until summer would give her a chance to recover and hopefully be ready to start school in the fall. We have a lot of praying, and reviewing our options, to do.

January 16 … I worked 8 to 5 today, and on my lunch break prepared my bag for the hospital, as I would be going straight from work. It started sleeting on the way over, so the roads were slick. I picked up dinner for Matthew and me, as he was with Emily.

When I got to the PICU, they were waiting for me to move her up to a regular floor! Progress is good. Emily had a new stuffed animal and didn't remember who gave it to her, but Matthew said she had it when he got there. I called John and he told me that he and Emily had been walking around the PICU. A short time later, the mother of another child who was there came to the room and said, "I have been here for two weeks with my daughter, and I have never seen a patient walking. Your daughter is beautiful and I wanted to get her something." What a testimony to where we have come from just a few days ago. During the darkest of those moments, I wondered if Emily would ever walk again.

January 17 ... Emily's favorite resident did rounds on her floor this morning right after breakfast. He was checking her vitals and as he was listening to her heart and lungs, he said, "I'm sorry, I probably have coffee breath." Without missing a beat, Emily replied, "That's ok, I probably have Froot Loop breath." What a character!

John came at noon so I could leave and be at work by 1 p.m. I called on my break and he said they were letting him bring Emily home! I couldn't believe it. I hope it's not too early after all she's been through.

January 19 ... When I tucked Emily in last night, I asked her what she thought about a second surgery and the timing of it. She said, "I don't like that I have to have another one, but I'd rather do it now and get it behind me and move on." I told her that I had talked to the guidance counselor at her school and that she felt we would be able to keep Emily on track with her class by continuing with homebound teachers after the school year ended until the work was completed—if there were no complications. Emily seemed pleased with that.

It is hard to focus on work with Emily at home. She's so close, yet I can't be there. It has been a month of an emotional roller coaster for me—and I hate roller coasters! Driving home from work, I sobbed the entire way. I'm exhausted, worried about another surgery, working full time, keeping up the house with cooking and cleaning, and trying to nurse Emily—with no skills at that whatsoever. I need one of those "Calgon, take me away" moments, but since that isn't going to happen, I dry my eyes and continue on.

January 23 … My mother-in-law had visitors from our church back in Minneapolis. I went down to see them and to share a bit about what we have been going through. They told me something a man in their church said after his three daughters had been killed in a tragic car accident: "It's more important to trust God than it is to understand Him." That resonated in my heart because that is exactly where I am. I have been asking so many "why" questions of God, and I knew at that point He was just saying, "Trust Me."

I got a call from the surgeon's office, making the appointment to see him again and to set the date for the next surgery: February 4.

Emily has gained 12 pounds in two weeks. Her pediatrician is concerned, but the endocrinologist isn't. She seems so puffy and feels uncomfortable.

January 29 … I worked half the day and then left to bring Emily to her appointment with the surgeon. There really wasn't any new information. He didn't feel like her memory loss would be re-affected, the sodium/fluid levels that still aren't totally stable will continue to be that way, and there is still a chance of stroke or seizure during surgery. He did not order another MRI. There have been people believing for the tumor to go away and feeling like we shouldn't schedule another surgery. While I know God could do it, there haven't been any indications that this has happened. It makes me wonder what those people would do if they were in the same situation in which we find ourselves.

February 3 ... Emily has been quiet the last few days and even more so today. She does things that don't require any interaction. She likes doing crossword and Sudoku puzzles.

We have been so blessed by some amazing meals brought by from friends and my next-door neighbor. Even though I had to work this afternoon, it's hard to focus, knowing that Emily is having a second brain surgery. She doesn't talk much about it and even though I have tried, she hasn't expressed her feelings about going through this again. I know I'm not prepared for this again, so I can't imagine how she could be! Unfortunately, now I know what to expect through the process: the waiting during surgery, the PICU, the recovery, and the list goes on.

CHAPTER 12

February 4 … 5 a.m. came early, but I would rather get up early and get things going than have to wait. I think it is easier on Emily, and not just mentally—since she can't eat before surgery, she doesn't have to get too hungry!

She finally was wheeled into the OR around 8:45 a.m. John put on the "suit" this time and walked back with her. He didn't get to go into the OR like I did. We received calls about every hour from a nurse who gave us updates on how she was doing. The surgeon, physician's assistant, and nurse came out around 1:30 p.m. to tell us everything had gone well. The surgeon again hugged us and said we could go down to the PICU and wait for them to call us back.

She didn't wake up until around 5 p.m., which made for a longer wait than after the last surgery. The incision is in the same location, but longer this time. The first thing she said when she woke up was, "My head hurts so badly." Imagine that! The nurse gave her some morphine.

John is going to stay tonight, so the rest of us came home. I began the phone calls while cleaning, starting laundry, and checking mail.

February 5 … I stayed home in the morning to get things caught up for the next couple days and ran some errands, one of them stopping at a jewelry store to get a watch battery changed. The store has organized a contest to win a piece of jewelry; I signed up for it without even looking at what I would win. I left for the hospital around noon.

Emily had already been moved out of the PICU to a regular floor! She looked good, but wasn't talking very much. She would nod or shake her head to answer yes-or-no questions. She was still very sleepy and wasn't eating, and had been nauseous.

The surgeon came to check on her and was pleased with her progress so far. I asked why the incision was so much bigger this time. He said, "I wanted to keep as much of the scarring in her hairline, so I had to make a larger cut to get to where I needed to go."

Our night nurse came in, and her countenance immediately caught my attention. She was bubbly and fun. Because she seemed young to be wearing reading glasses, I asked her why she had them. She told us that when she was 22 and in her last year of nursing school, she found out that she had leukemia. She said she had received treatment and beaten the disease, but that a lingering side effect was a need for reading glasses. She also went on to say, "You know, I wouldn't wish that disease on anyone, but I used it to turn my life around. I embraced life and I finished my degree and now I give back to others as much as I can."

I'm sure she had no idea what an impact her story had on Emily and me. She proceeded to draw a report card on the whiteboard and asked Emily to "grade" the day nurse. She made Emily laugh, which hadn't happened in several days.

We received an email from a missionary whom John met on a mission trip with our church to Central America. He wrote that he had heard about Emily and, after praying for her, felt prompted to email us. He wrote, "What kind of a Shepherd would send His sheep out among wolves, but One who had supreme confidence that He could take great care of them in the midst of that reality." He added, "The day will come when you will win! That day will come because you are loved by God and He is inviting you to rest in His great love." What an encouragement at a low point for us.

February 6 … Emily had a good night, even though she had blood draws every three hours. Her sodium levels stabilized. We waited all day for the MRI results from yesterday, until the surgeon came by around 6:30 p.m. He said there was no evidence of the tumor on the MRI! He said we would re-scan in three months because there was a chance of recurrence, but all I heard was "tumor free." Even though it has only been two months, it has seemed like years with all we have been through.

The endocrinologist came by and told us that Emily's puffiness is because she is retaining water. That doesn't make much sense because for five hours during the night, she went to the bathroom every 30 minutes. She was still hooked up to machines, so I would have to unplug her every time she went. Her body is not holding on to the fluids she is taking in.

February 7 ... Morning came early because we got very little sleep last night. I helped Emily take a shower. That first shower after surgery is the worst. Her hair had once again been braided, and the blood and "goop" from surgery had matted it all together. I had her take pain medication first in order for the pain to not be as bad. The water ran red for some time before I even tried to put on the shampoo. Rinsing took a while, but we finished just as John was arriving. I had to be at work by 1 p.m.

While at work a bit later, John called and said they were discharging her. As much as I want her at home, I'm not at all sure she is ready to be out of the hospital—but then again, what do I know?

February 8 ... John slept in Emily's room. (It was his turn.) I have gotten into the habit of leaving my cell phone turned on 24/7, and at 3 a.m. I got a call from John (from upstairs in Emily's bedroom), that she had thrown up everywhere and on everything and he needed help cleaning up. "Everywhere" described it well. I stripped the bed, blankets, and comforter and then put on clean sheets and blankets. I helped her bathe, started the laundry, and went back to bed, only to get up a couple hours later for work.

When I came home on my break, she was sleeping. At 4:30 the hospital called and said she needed to be brought back in as soon as possible, as her last blood draw was dangerously low. John brought her to the ER and the next sodium check remained the same, even after she had received fluids. They did a CT scan, which showed everything to be normal. The endocrinologist came by late and said he thought she had developed a rare "cranium sodium dump," which he described as a condition in which her body is trying to get rid of all the sodium that is stored. They once again admitted her.

Enough already! On top of the latest developments with Emily, I was told at work that I was performing below target and I need to be at least on target. I honestly don't know when I have felt more beaten-down in every area of my life. Will it ever end?

CHAPTER 13

February 9 … I ran some errands at home and made a nice breakfast for Andrew, Matthew, and Sarah before heading up to the hospital. Emily's sodium levels had stabilized once again, but she was back to where her reasoning and thought processes were off. I know from before that it is most likely from the fluid shifts going on, but I hope we don't go back to the brain stem issue again. The stress of all of this is affecting everyone, and we are all on edge with one another. Patience and longsuffering are not in our vocabulary right now; I think we've all reached our personal limits on this maximum dose of stress!

February 10 … Emily is very quiet and almost serene. She only speaks when spoken to, and then only in short answers. The left side of her face is a little droopy, and she still is unable to process information clearly. Matthew came up after lunch and it was so nice to have him there, for someone else to talk to and also to try to engage Emily in conversation.

My older sister was traveling on business within a couple hours of here, so she flew in a day early to see us. She and

I went to get some dinner and brought back some extra-special macaroni and cheese for Emily. Normally, that would have made her day, but today it did very little to lift her spirits.

February 11 ... The hospital released Emily—is it too soon again? I also had a message on my phone from the jewelry store to call them. I called them back and they told me I had won the prize that I had registered for and to come pick it up. I drove over and found a beautiful necklace that was similar to the one being given away in the swag bags to the presenters at the Country Music Awards, along with a handmade box of gourmet chocolates in an edible chocolate box! I was so overwhelmed by this lovely gift when I never win anything!

February 15 ... We have made a couple of visits for blood draws, but haven't gotten any results back. She has been doing okay, though, so there's reason to hope for the best.

I had to work from 1 to 10 p.m., and since there was Valentine's banquet at church, John took Sarah; John's mother was coming to stay with Emily and play games. I was at work when I got a call from home saying that Emily had passed out with Grandma there, and that John was on the way to the hospital.

Meanwhile, we had store inventory, which I was supposed to coordinate. This "event" is always so stressful anyway, and I was thinking of the life of my daughter at the hospital and couldn't really take time to call and find out what was going on. I left the store at 1:30 a.m., completely exhausted.

I assured my boss on our way out that I can handle the business side of things and do what is needed of me at the store … but can I?

John called me on the way home from the ER to tell me that the sodium levels are extremely low and that she is doing the sodium-dumping thing again.

February 16 … It is a Saturday, so the pediatrician's office was open in the morning. I took her in and the doctor drew the blood. The pediatrician told us she had been in contact with the endocrinologist and they both feel that Emily is experiencing cerebral sodium waste, with her body trying to rid itself of all its sodium. But some sodium is a good thing—it just has to be balanced.

The doctors both feel that we need to stick with original medication plan at least for the weekend and then re-evaluate. It is important at this point to get her stabilized.

She slept for a while when we got home. Later in the day, everyone else had something going on, so I told her we were going to have a "girls' night." I gave her a facial and we watched a movie together. I'd like to say that we were making memories, but she won't remember any of it.

February 18 … We had a day off from lab work yesterday, but today we were back—the endocrinologist had ordered the labs to be drawn. Once we got called back into a room, we were told that these were more extensive than they could do in the office, and that we would have to go to the hospital. The routine lab work turned complicated, and 2½ hours later, we finally made it back home.

Emily was exhausted. She was puffy and looked flushed. We got the call from the doctor that the levels were still very low. Every two hours, around the clock, she has to take one-gram sodium tablets to compensate for all the sodium her body is getting rid of.

February 19 … I slept in Emily's room and set my clock to give her the sodium pills. Within 45 minutes of her taking the pill, she started throwing up—violently. I changed the bedding and got her cleaned up, but couldn't go back to sleep. Everything always seems worse at night. This sodium imbalance is getting the best of me—why won't it stabilize, and when will this end?

John took Emily for labs because I had to go to work. The pediatrician was very concerned because the sodium levels dropped another 5 points. The endocrinologist was notified, and we are to take her to see him tomorrow.

February 20 … Emily's labs this morning were much higher … but now the fear is that they rose too fast. She didn't feel well at all today, and by the time I got home from work, she had really declined. She couldn't remember who the President is or her brother's middle name. She started crying in frustration because she knew that those were questions she should know the answers to.

We called the endocrinologist and he said to bring her to the ER. That was the second 45-minute trip to the hospital in one day. John took her because I had to work, and we didn't know if they would admit her. They gave her fluids and sent her home around 2 a.m. Emily's favorite resident happened to be doing his time tonight in the ER, so that was a bright spot. It is strange what a "bright spot" looks like when life is turned upside down!

February 22 … The afternoon sodium check yesterday showed stabilization. I slept in Emily's room because John had been up the night before. She had a "breakthrough" from 2 to 6 a.m., going to the bathroom every 15 to 20 minutes. This was somewhat worrisome because it could cause the sodium to become unbalanced again.

I took her for labs around 9 a.m. and then Sarah, Emily, and I went to get breakfast to wait for the results. On the way home, Emily noticed a "For Sale" sign on a friend's house. (It has been for sale for about two months.) She had forgotten that the parents had separated and that her friend had moved out with her mother. She started crying because of how upsetting it was to her to not remember—it truly is a loss.

When we got the lab results back, they were elevated again. My heart aches for my daughter, who just wants things to get back to normal.

February 24 … Yesterday Emily's sodium was still high, but the doctor didn't seem too concerned. We have to continue keeping track of her "ins and outs." Her outs today were right at five liters! She basically just drinks to keep up with how much she goes to the bathroom.

I heard a song on Christian radio today that had the line, "It's all about You, Jesus ... " I totally fell apart in the car while driving and listening. As much as I surrender to the ways of the Lord, I just don't understand why this continues. Emily is still very quiet and seems somewhat despondent.

February 26 ... The endocrinologist stopped the sodium tablets because the levels have been on the high side. It was a relief, as they can make her so sick—but the relief was short-lived.

John called me at work at 7 p.m. to say he was on his way to the ER with Emily. Sure enough, there was a significant drop in sodium, so the tablets returned.

I returned home from work to find a letter from a well-meaning person asking if there was something (e.g., bitterness, unforgiveness, etc.) in our lives that we hadn't dealt with that could be causing this affliction. Thinking that I had issues that were the cause of the hell we, and especially Emily, were dealing with, was more than I could imagine. I processed it as best as I could.

The scripture I read was Psalm 139:5, 12: "Thou hast enclosed me behind and before ... even the darkness is not too dark for Thee."

CHAPTER 14

March 2 … Went to church for the first time since December! Everyone was so happy to see Emily. We only stayed for the worship because she got very tired. I noticed how her large motor skills are messed up—she wasn't even able to clap on beat.

March 4 … We had a follow-up visit with the surgeon today. He said that her memory could take up to six months to return and may not ever come back completely. He hadn't realized that she'd had so many complications. He had known about the diabetes insipidus, but not the cranial sodium waste. He was very surprised that her vision had come back so well because he really hadn't expected it to.

March 13 … Emily was able to start school with homebound teachers. Because her memory is still such an issue, they teach her the content and give her quizzes and tests the same day because she won't remember it the next day. Both teachers are incredibly patient, and one of them is coming every day after school. We have gone several days with blood samples being normal!

April 28 … The several days has now been several weeks of normal blood samples. Emily continues to work diligently on school and on getting back into "life." We saw the endocrinologist today, and he is going to let us see if her pituitary gland is working at all. We will wean her off two of the three medications.

I am massaging her feet every day in the area where the nerve ending for the pituitary gland function is. A neighbor who is a massage therapist showed me the chart where all the organs of the body have stimulation points. We have a month for God to work to return her body to produce everything on its own.

May 10 … As I was massaging Emily's feet and head (she had a terrible headache), I just kept thinking, "When will this nightmare end?" The thought came to me of just how special Emily is. Obviously I'm her mother and so I would naturally think that, but she has handled everything so well. I felt like the Lord must think she is pretty special, too! The Book of Job indicates that God allowed Satan to test Job— because He knew Job could handle the test! Job lost much during the testing, but came out ahead in the end because the Lord blessed him beyond his comprehension. That is what I am believing for Emily.

June 5 … We got lab results back and they showed that her pituitary gland isn't producing or doing anything. We have to start back on all her medications immediately. I am saddened and disappointed. I was so confident that the pituitary gland would function. In the Book of Luke, the Angel said to Mary, "All things are possible" (Luke 1:37).

The positive note on the day is that Emily's homebound teacher said that the end of school is in sight, and she will be able to finish with her class!

July 7 … Some dear friends blessed Emily, Sarah, and me with frequent-flier tickets to California. John's sister and her family live in Los Angeles. We spent an amazing 10 days thinking the worst was behind us.

Emily has always wanted to visit the Jelly Belly Factory, since that is one of her favorite kinds of candy. We rode cable cars, saw the Golden Gate Bridge, and walked down Lombard Street. It was a fabulous time that we will remember for the rest of our lives.

It was hard to see Emily get so tired from a day of sightseeing, but we filled every day with wonderful food and touring the city. (Note: Little did we know how important those memories would be.)

July 18 … Emily saw the eye specialist today. He had seen her a couple months ago and said her vision was 20/40. This time he said it was 20/160. He said it must have been wrong the first time, and that she just needed glasses.

July 21 … Emily went to the optometrist she had first seen when her eyes were bad before the surgeries. She said Emily's vision is now 20/200 and, once again, glasses won't help—though frames would at least protect her eyes.

July 26 … The endocrinologist has recommended starting Emily on human growth hormone shots. Her growth plate is still open, and the thought process is that if she can get some height before she starts estrogen, it will help her with the weight gain as well. A nurse came to the house today to show Emily how to use the machine. It's pretty cool! It is also supposed to give her more energy.

August 18 … The girls started school. Emily was nervous and excited. Her memory is still an issue because she can't remember her locker combination and where each of her classes is located, but she finally feels like she can get her life back to normal and be a regular teenager. I am hoping that repetition will help with the class changes. She is good at writing everything down so she can remember it later.

August 20 … Emily came home and said it is difficult for her to see the board at school. I emailed all of her teachers to request that she be moved closer to the board.

I found out from a friend who teaches at school that one of the teachers asked Emily what was wrong with her because she couldn't remember where her classes were. I was furious! Apparently, so were some other teachers once they heard about it, because the teacher apologized to

Emily the next day. Emily has a truly admirable capacity to overlook such an offense. The short-term memory loss can also be a blessing when she doesn't remember being wronged!

August 26 … The teacher who spoke harshly to Emily came to my store today and apologized for what she said to her. The school called and talked about the possibility of getting a special education classification for Emily that would allow her to have extra time to do assignments because of her memory. When I asked Emily what she thought about it, she said, "I just don't know. There's so much and I feel so overwhelmed." She started crying gently at first, then started sobbing and said, "I wish this had never happened." She failed a geometry quiz today and is really concerned.

August 27 … It seems like her eyes have worsened overnight. She is holding printed material and looking at the computer about 10 inches away from her. I'm desperately trying not to think the worst, but it's hard not to.

August 28 … I called the neurosurgeon's office this morning about what was going on and they scheduled an MRI for this afternoon. It was a quiet drive to the hospital, with each of us lost in our own thoughts. I helped her study when we got home. She is really struggling and got an "F" on a Spanish quiz today.

CHAPTER 15

August 29 … I had gotten to work early and was doing paperwork before we opened when my cell phone buzzed. I saw it was the P.A. for our surgeon. I answered, and I heard it in her voice before I heard what she said. "The tumor has grown back. I am so sorry." She said they had already scheduled surgery for Tuesday, the day after Labor Day. She wanted us to come in later to go over everything with the doctor.

I called John, who happened to be at the bedside of an older woman in our church who was dying of brain cancer, to tell him the news. Sobbing, I called my boss and told her. She told me I needed to go home, as another manager was coming in. She then proceeded to pick me up and take me for a strong cup of coffee, and to buy an amazing chocolate cake! She said that chocolate helps everything seem a bit better.

The next couple hours were surreal as I tried to comprehend what was happening. I went to pick up Emily from school. I just told her we had a doctor's appointment, wanting to wait until I got her home, with John, to tell her the news. She stopped at her locker to drop books off and wondered which ones she should bring home. I tried to be nonchalant, but inside I thought to myself that it could be a while before she'd be back at school again.

John was home when we arrived, and we all sat down on our couch and we told her the news. She started crying and just said, "Again?"

At the appointment with the surgeon, the MRI showed that the tumor is in the same location as the first time, although only one-third the size. He told us that because her vision has deteriorated so quickly, he is going to be as aggressive as possible to save her sight, which could mean another surgery if he doesn't get the whole tumor. He explained that the incision will be the biggest one yet, and that she will have more swelling around her eyes.

Emily was quiet during the appointment and on the way home. I played a game with her this evening to help take her mind off of it, even a little.

August 31 … Emily came to me this morning asking the same question: "Do you think I have done something that made this happen again?" I scooped her in my arms and assured her that that was absolutely not the case!

The church service this morning was good, and some dear friends took us out for lunch at a favorite Japanese restaurant afterward. Later this afternoon, a good friend of mine called and talked to Emily, telling her that she wished she could have the surgery in her place. (This is a woman who has had over 50 surgeries in her life!) Emily's response to her was, "That's okay, I wouldn't let you."

September 2 ... Some dates become cemented in one's mind because of certain events—this is one of them. The surgery was delayed until noon, which meant a long morning of waiting—and for Emily, not eating. She went in and, unfortunately, we now knew the routine all too well.

We got the usual hourly updates before the surgeon came out and, again, reported being pleased with how well everything went.

In recovery, it took Emily a lot longer to wake up this time. She was very restless, as well as nauseous and in a lot of pain. When she finally woke up, she couldn't see anything. The P.A. checked on her and felt that it was due to swelling from the surgery and ordered an MRI to make sure everything looked okay. It did.

The surgeon did his rounds and said it could be a number of things: trauma and shock from surgery, nerves being out of place, or, because her vision had been so compromised, a permanent condition. I struggled to remain calm and to keep Emily's spirits up and the mood light.

Our favorite resident came in to check on her and asked us if he could pray with us and for Emily. It was very sweet and meant so much to us. Emily tries so hard to be stoic, but she is really having a hard time and it breaks my heart to see her like this.

I found the small chapel in the hospital and, finding it empty, poured my heart out to the Lord on behalf of my daughter. Thankfully I was alone in my grief, because my sobbing was not very ladylike. I know God has a plan for

Emily, but right now I have to wonder if that plan allows her to see with her natural eyes.

My dear friend from Wisconsin had told me to call her anytime, and I felt impressed that now would be a good time. She picked up the phone and, through my nearly incoherent sobbing, I told her what had happened. She said that their church leaders were at their home and asked if it was okay to put me on speaker and have them join in prayer for Emily right now. It was a powerful and moving time of prayer and I felt the strength of the Lord in the midst of the "dark" time we are in.

September 4 … Emily woke up this morning and her eyes were almost swollen shut. Her whole face was swollen. Doctors examined her and didn't really say anything new. She was very quiet and contemplative. I read from the book of Psalms to her before I had to leave to go to work. It took everything in me to leave. I cried during the entire drive home. I am claiming Exodus 14:15 that says, "Stand and SEE the salvation of the Lord."

Five different eye specialists examined her today. The final determination is that the blood vessels that carry blood to the eyes have been damaged by the tumor. The vision loss is permanent. Our surgeon said that there is a small chance that with another surgery, he could try to increase the blood flow. But he explained that it was more dangerous going back into surgery only two days after the last one, because of the higher risk of infection and also of her having a stroke.

Really, what choice do we have? I called several friends who cried with me and prayed with me for a miracle.

September 5 … Surgery was scheduled for 2 p.m. John, Emily, and I were together before she had to go, and we shared a sweet time of prayer together. She didn't seem scared, just maybe a bit apprehensive. How does a 15-year-old prepare for a life of blindness in her mind?

Our favorite resident came in and gave us a scripture he had written out for Emily. He read it to her and said that it was one that always brought comfort to him when he was in a tough situation. Ps. 91:1 says, "He who dwells in the shelter of the Most High will abide under the shadow of the Almighty." Matthew came and we tried to keep the atmosphere light until we kissed her and said good-bye around 1:45. Then the three of us just started sobbing, and the waiting began.

The hourly reports were good—that everything was going fine. At 6:15 p.m., the surgeon came out and said that everything had gone well. He also said, "Everything looks the way it did when God created her."

I came home and made all the phone calls to update everyone. My brother-in-law in California summed it up perfectly: "Emily brings out the best in all of us."

September 6 … John called to say that her eyes were tracking as well as dilating and constricting, although she was still unable to see. She gets so weary of all the checking. When I got to the hospital so John could leave, I met the

P.A. and she told me that sometimes the brain will trick a person into thinking they can see, when in reality they can't.

Our music minister and his wife came and prayed over her specifically that the Lord would reveal Himself to her and that the encounter would be tangible and real. There was a moment when she held her hand up in front of her and she said she could see the outline! We were all beside ourselves with joy!

September 7 … Emily had a very restless night. She was also disoriented. Part of this is due to the fact that she has no concept of night and day outside of us telling her. The eye exams today revealed that nothing has changed and that what she "saw" was all in her mind.

September 8 … I had a rough day at work and then went up to the hospital. Emily wanted to take a shower. I began the laborious and tedious job of once again unbraiding and detangling her bloodied hair. This time was the worst, with the two surgeries back to back.

She sat on a stool in the shower and I just let the water flow through her hair and over her. She said it felt so good. I had just finished and was getting the towels when she felt nauseous and faint. I couldn't reach the nurse's call button, and she wasn't able to sit up. I was so scared that she was going to pass out—she was very pale and weak. But after a few minutes, I was able to get her to the bed and call a nurse to help. When I explained the episode to the doctors, none of them had any idea what had happened—

comforting thought. Dear friends from Minnesota, Wisconsin, and Colorado are all calling with their thoughts and prayers.

September 9 … The blood draw this morning showed very high sodium levels. The IV was taken out yesterday, so that means Emily has to drink in order for it to come down. She has handled it okay.

I took her for a walk around the unit. She is still unsteady from getting used to her blindness. As we were walking, she said to me, "You know, the one thing I've learned through this is to just accept things that you have no control over and can't change." That was a pretty profound statement from a 15-year-old girl who has been blind for seven days.

Emily had more vision testing today, lasting three hours. The nerves and muscles aren't tracking at all, and the blood vessels carrying blood to her eyes are thin—meaning they are dying. She had gone two days without blood flowing to her eyes, and the doctor feels that had been too long, that the damage was permanent.

This evening after dinner, Emily opened up about some of her fears. She said hesitantly, "What if I don't see again?" I looked at her and I said, "Emily, we will handle it with grace and dignity. I will be your eyes." It's like I could see the wheels moving in her head: How will I finish school, go to college, get a job, have a family? I think about those things, too—my heart breaks over her loss.

Emily had yet another MRI late today. It was almost 8 p.m. A friend stopped by as Emily was leaving to have the test, and stayed with me for the duration of it. She has also been one of Emily's homebound teachers. She said the impact of what Emily has been through, and is going through, is great at her school. The general consensus of everyone is that she is incredibly brave.

September 10 ... Emily had eaten breakfast and was sitting up in the bed. She actually looked radiant and very sweet! All of a sudden she turned toward me and said, "God is so good."

I was taken aback and didn't quite know how to respond, but said, "I agree, but what makes you say that?" She replied, "It's just so amazing that when you lose one of your senses, God makes the other ones stronger. I can already hear better." I immediately agreed and was struck by the fact that the Lord is ministering to her spirit and giving her His peace—which the Word says passes ALL understanding (Philippians 4:7)! She may be worried about her future, but she is accepting it, whatever package it may come in.

An occupational therapist came by to teach her some techniques to use in dealing with the blindness, such as how to fill a glass, how to eat, and how to use a sighted guide. It was surreal, sitting there listening and watching as this woman instructed my daughter, who is blind, on how to function in that capacity.

I had to leave to go to work and, of course, the surgeon came right after I left. He just repeated what we knew. The tumor had compromised the blood vessels so much, by reducing the flow of blood to the eyes, that once it was removed they couldn't compensate for the loss.

I still sobbed after hearing that because of the finality of it. I can be strong when I am with Emily, for her sake, but when I am alone the floodgates are wide open. I feel as if my life is out of control and there is nothing I can do to change the progress. I am holding on to the scripture that says, "The Lord is my strength and my Strong Tower" (Proverbs 18:10). I am running to the Tower!

September 11 ... Obviously, this date will forever be significant for us as Americans. For me personally, I feel like the "chief terrorist" (i.e., the Enemy) has attacked our "tower" (i.e., the Trade Towers), meaning my family unit. God has already promised that He will be victorious, and I am claiming that victory for us!

Emily was released from the hospital today. This was her longest stay—nine days. She does seem stronger both mentally and physically this time, though. Thankfully her memory wasn't affected at all, which is huge.

As soon as she got home, she wanted to know what she could do to help with dinner preparations. I had her set the table for me. She is getting around the house with no problems at all. The rest of us have to be mindful about leaving doors open and leaving items on the floor.

September 12 ... In conversation with my sister, she gave me the contact information for a pediatric ophthalmologist at Emory University Hospital in Atlanta. It took me several hours to get the required referrals and an appointment, but we do have an appointment for a second opinion.

Emily is going to the bathroom a lot, which means we are going to have sodium issues. I really don't think I can handle the diabetes insipidus on top of the blindness.

September 17 … I've been talking to the school about setting up homebound teaching as well as a vision teacher—one who will teach Emily Braille. This is a new experience for all of us, and we all have agreed that the way we start may have to be modified.

I've also talked to the Human Resources Department at my company and found out that there is a "PTO Bank" I can tap into, since I have used up all my vacation days. I am proposing to work four days a week so I have an extra day for appointments and meetings at school.

September 24 … We traveled to Emory today. We were eating lunch and I looked up and there was a sign on a business signboard that read, "Prayer Changes Things." What an encouragement!

While we were eating, Emily started feeling weak in her limbs and experiencing shortness of breath. She had difficulty lifting her arms. I have no idea what that's all about, but I'm pretty sure an ophthalmologist won't know!

There was a Trader Joe's close to the hospital and since we don't have one nearby, I wanted to stop. I was checking out and in conversation told the cashier that I was taking my daughter to Emory. He paused and said, "Wait just a minute." He grabbed a bouquet of flowers and handed them to me, saying, "I hope she'll be okay and that these will cheer her up." The flowers were named "stargazers." I am so hopeful that she will be able to gaze up at the stars again, and the thoughtfulness of that cashier was overwhelming.

Two residents examined Emily first and asked a lot of questions. Then the specialist came in and examined her as well. She finished and made a facial gesture, silently asking us if she should talk in front of Emily. We told her Emily understands everything that is going on.

She said that while craniopharyngiomas are usually benign, they are sticky because they have no cell wall and damage everything around them. She said there was nerve and retina damage and, for that reason, medical advancements probably wouldn't help Emily "in her lifetime." She explained that in studies with monkeys, their vision loss was permanent after only 45 minutes with lack of blood flow. Emily's had been two days before they tried to correct it.

It was a long and quiet drive home, each one of us wrapped up in our own thoughts. Emily was exhausted. While part of me wasn't surprised by the doctor's words, the other part of me wanted them to be able to "do" something, partially because I am at such a loss to do anything to help Emily. Thankfully we know that "with God, ALL things are possible" (Matthew 19:26).

September 25 … I had to work 8 to 5, and John really needed to go into the office after missing yesterday while being at Emory. I made sure that Andrew was going to be home with her for the time that we would be gone. She said, "I hate being a bother." She thinks that we are going out of our way to make sure she is all settled, and that it is a bother. I assured her that wasn't the case, but I can just see it weighing heavily on her mind.

It is very difficult to separate work from what is going on at home. Many times I cry all the way to work, take a deep breath, wipe my eyes, and walk in to the store, to put it behind me for eight hours. Then someone I know will come in and ask about Emily. It's not like I can say, "Oh, she's fine," or give a 10-second response. It's a little exhausting. Sometimes I wish that I had the option of running away or falling apart.

October 2 … We had a meeting at school to establish Emily's IEP (Individual Education Plan). She now falls under the "Special Education" category at school. The three teachers who will do homebound teaching were there, as well as her Braille teacher and her case manager from the Commission for the Blind. The teachers will all be coming to the house for the next couple of months, and then we will transition her into school for the second half of the school year.

CHAPTER 16

October 14 ... Emily's vision teacher brought a Perkins Brailler to the house. This is a typewriter-like machine that types in Braille. She seems to be catching on to Braille, although she knows she has a long way to go to feel comfortable with it.

A friend gave Emily the audio book *The Shack*. We've been listening to it together, and today we listened to the portion that said, "The great sadness lifted." The author knew that Jesus was always there, and He caused it to lift.

The book has been so good for me in many ways. I have wanted my "moment" with God to ask Him "WHY," just like the character in the book was given the opportunity. I know that I can continue to ask the questions, and that my God is big enough to handle them.

I have noticed that Emily doesn't seem to be able to smell. We could put a strong scent up to her nose, and there is nothing. I asked the surgeon about it and he said that loss of smell was a "typical" side effect from the type of surgery that she had. Now she is only able to utilize three of her five senses.

October 15 … Two of Emily's teachers came to the house to administer the PSAT. This test took her five hours, as it all had to be done orally. They were all exhausted after it was over!

Emily had her first O&M (Orientation and Mobility) lesson today with her teacher from the South Carolina School for the Blind. She will be "fitted" with a white folding cane, sized to her height, but until then she has a straight cane to get used to. She doesn't like it at all and would much rather use a "sighted guide."

October 31 … Sarah, Emily, and I traveled 2½ hours to attend a conference with the speaker Jennifer Rothschild. We had loved her humor, sensitivity, and encouragement in her book, *Lessons I Learned in the Dark*. We had come across this book at the exact time that we needed to hear her message of hope. Jennifer began losing her sight around the same age as Emily.

Because of Emily's blindness, we were ushered to front row seats, and Emily was able to meet Jennifer during a break and have a picture taken with her! Emily was thrilled!

When we got home that day, I got a call from a friend in Minnesota who told me she had nominated Emily's name to the Make-A-Wish Foundation. The surgeon was contacted, and after all the paperwork, we received a letter from the South Carolina chapter that she was accepted and would be granted a wish. We went online and read a little about what she might be able to do.

November 5 … The volunteers from Make-A-Wish came to the house and explained the program to her and what she might wish for. Her options were:

Be Someone … Meet Someone … Get Something … Go Somewhere …

They asked her if she had any ideas, and I think she was so awestruck at the possibilities that she said she would have to think about it. Her eyes were so big as they gave her ideas to choose from.

November 10 … We invited the volunteers over so Emily could tell them her wish. She wants to go to New York City and see the Broadway musical *The Lion King*. She loves the story and the music from when she was little and can picture it in her head. They love her idea and said they will submit it for approval.

She also requested that our family could go as part of the wish. She knows that her family has been a part of the last year of her life, with all the ups and downs.

They also asked her many questions about what she liked in order to add experiences to the trip. She of course said that she loves chocolate and macaroni and cheese!

As I was putting her to bed, she seemed unusually quiet. I thought maybe it was from all the excitement of the events of the day. I asked her if anything was wrong and she said, "I am so scared to go back to school, of being alone in life because no one will want to marry me, and if something happens to you and Dad." I had tears streaming down my face as she talked and I just listened. I was afraid, too, and all I know to do is to pray for a peace to flood her spirit and for her to know that somehow God is in control.

November 12 ... We had another IEP at school today, and the plan is finalized. Emily will return to school for half days at the beginning of the second semester. The school district will provide her with a laptop computer that has "talking" software installed, and the Commission for the Blind will provide calculators and other manipulatives that she can use. She will have a teacher's aide with her at all times to assist going from class to class and to help her with note-taking in the classroom.

Emily spoke up and voiced her fears of going back. Everyone was understanding and very supportive. I know that they will do everything in their power to make this transition as easy for Emily as they can.

November 18 ... Emily had a routine MRI today and an appointment with the surgeon. He told us that there is a spot, and that he cannot be sure if it is scar tissue or a tumor. He recommended a procedure called "Gamma Knife," which is a non-invasive approach with low doses of radiation. This is possible because the spot is still small—grape size. He also told us that he is moving in two months!

We met one of Emily's favorite nurses up on her floor after the appointment. She was so encouraging, telling Emily that she's been such a "gift" to her, and that she continues to be amazed at how well Emily continues to handle everything.

In Jennifer Rothschild's book, *Lessons I Learned in the Dark*, she talks about how she chose to receive her blindness as a "gift." It is a perspective that is hard to take, but one that will allow us all to view this with an anticipation of what God can do with us. I feel like Emily will choose that as well, in time.

November 20 … Emily's homebound geometry teacher is trying to encourage her in her return to school. She has talked to the class Emily is going to be in and has given the students Emily's email address. Emily has been so happy to receive contact from them. This teacher is also planning a Christmas assembly for the last day of school before the Christmas break and would like Emily to share a little about her experience. I would say that Emily is open to the idea, but has not totally embraced it.

November 21 … I heard about a world-renowned pediatric neurosurgeon from Johns Hopkins University, Dr. Ben Carson. I got his address and sent him some of Emily's records for a second opinion. I received word from him today that there is nothing else that he could do for her.

Sometimes I think I should be used to, and immune to, the disappointment, but the pain is still there when I hear that there is no hope.

I took Emily to school right before lunch to meet the kids who have been emailing her. Many said hello, and one girl in particular (whom Emily hadn't known very well before) was very attentive and engaged her in conversation.

On the way home, I asked her how she felt. She said. "Everyone was nice, but the thought of going back is still so overwhelming."

December 1 ... My district manager came to my store today to let us know that our location would be closing permanently on January 31. So now on top of the worst year of my life, I am losing my job! As stressful and difficult as my job is at times, I have great health insurance, which now is a priority and a necessity. I have the option to transfer to a "sister" store, but that would mean a 45- to 60-minute commute, one way. The scripture that keeps going through my mind is that "All things work together for good" (Romans 8:28).

December 3 ... We got the call from the Make-A-Wish volunteers that EVERY part of the wish was granted! Our whole family is going to New York City! The timing of this couldn't be better. The volunteers will be coming in a few days to go over everything with us. We are going to try to go around New Year's, while the kids are still out of school.

December 7 ... One year ago today, we got the news that would change our lives forever. Four surgeries later, and with Emily's permanent vision loss, we are now faced with a perspective that we never thought we would be dealing with. What we are blessed with is the fact that Emily is alive! She continues to touch the hearts of all those with whom she comes in contact.

Emily and I watched a movie on TV about a man who had Tourette's syndrome and didn't let it stop him from his dream of being a teacher. His mother believed in him. The story hit pretty close to home, and I sobbed through much of it as I realized the mountains that Emily would have to scale in order to fulfill her dreams.

Will she have the stamina do climb those mountains? Will she want to give up? Will she always have the support system she needs?

I am struck by the fact that she and I both must take one day at a time in this new adventure. If we start to look at the big picture, it will be far too overwhelming. But one day at a time? We can do that!

CHAPTER 17

December 15 ... Today, Emily had the Gamma Knife procedure. We were at the hospital by 9 a.m., but ended up waiting until 11 for her to go back. They drilled four tiny holes in her head and then secured a "halo-like" apparatus on her. She then had another MRI, and then a team of doctors pinpointed exactly where the tumor was and at what angle the radiation would come in. It is a highly technical procedure.

The surgeon called around 2 p.m. to tell us that it was over and everything went well. She ended up doing so well in recovery that she was discharged and didn't have to spend the night as planned!

Now comes the real waiting. Because the doses of radiation are so small, it could take one to two years before the full extent of the procedure is realized. So, we hope and pray for the best.

Emily decided tonight that she is going to share her story at the school assembly, and called her teacher to let her know. She and I have written it out, with both of us sharing certain details.

December 18 … Emily was so nervous on the drive out to school. We prayed for a peace and a calmness to envelop her. We saw that we were last on the program, which meant a longer time to feel nervous. Emily had to memorize her portions, which is difficult with her memory. There were about 800 students and teachers in the school gym. We got up to speak, and the auditorium got silent as we began.

There were some emotional parts, with a bit of humor thrown in. I said, "My daughter is going to be coming back to school after the break to a building that is totally dark to her. I want you all to know what happened to her and that she is the same person she was before, only unable to see. I want you to know that this is Emily, instead of 'that blind kid.'" When we finished, we received a standing ovation, and I had all I could do to keep from falling apart from the emotion of the moment.

Many students, teachers, and the principal came up to Emily and said how much what she said had meant to them. Many said that even though they hadn't known her before, they admired her courage and it would make them better people after hearing her share. A newspaper reporter was there and asked us afterward if we would be willing to have her do a piece for the paper on Emily's story.

December 25 … I have to say, the thought certainly crossed my mind that it would be pretty awesome if Emily woke up Christmas morning able to see. We all tried to explain everything to her so she wouldn't feel like she was missing out. She has such a positive attitude.

I went for a walk in between the big breakfast I always make on Christmas and the dinner later in the day. I was praying and asking God, "It's okay if You don't answer all my questions, but please just give me some assurance that everything is going to be okay."

December 29 … The Wish volunteers came after I got home from work to explain everything and go over the paperwork. We will be staying at a hotel in Times Square, and because of the things Emily said she liked, they had given us an amazing itinerary for our time there! Her eyes were huge as they were explaining everything to us! She will even have some spending money, which she is thrilled about!

December 31 … What a year this has been … I wrote in my journal last January 1 that I hoped 2008 would be a better year than the way 2007 had ended. That certainly didn't happen. We have been on a journey unlike any we could have ever imagined.

The girls and I went shopping to try to find a dress for Emily for New York and finally found one. I helped Emily pack for the trip. She was tired early and didn't think she could make it to midnight. I was praying with her, when she started praying. "Thank you Lord for the friends you are going to bring into my life and for the things that You will accomplish through me because of this disability. Help me to walk through the doors that only You can open that wouldn't be there if it wasn't for this happening in my life. In Jesus' Name, Amen." The insight she has is amazing.

Everyone else was either gone or busy with something, so I watched the ball drop in Times Square all alone, amazed that I would be there in a couple days. Then I sobbed my way into another year, remembering that it is exactly how I "brought" in 2008.

January 2, 2009 ... A limousine picked us up at our house at 5 a.m. for the hour-long drive to the airport—what a way to go! And after our flight, we got picked up at LaGuardia by another limo for our drive into the city.

We were there too early for our rooms to be ready, so we stored our bags and went to find lunch and look around Times Square. How do I explain everything to Emily? New York City is full of sounds, but the sights make up so much of it. I did the best I could, and she seemed to be able to grasp it to some extent.

The girls and I walked Fifth Avenue to see the holiday windows, which was a dream we have always shared. Emily couldn't "see" them, but the cool thing was that many of them had music that coincided with the windows, so she "heard" them.

Emily was pretty tired after a very long day, so she took a bath to warm up and went to bed early. She keeps saying how everything is so "cool," and she is so excited to be here.

January 3 ... Emily loves chocolate, and the Wish people knew that, so we had a tour of chocolate factory. We had the most amazing hot chocolate ever while waiting for the owner to help us make chocolate! The owner was wonderful with Emily, especially, and all of us got to make chocolates. Then we had a tasting time at the end with several different flavors. He sent us off with four huge bags of chocolate—interesting to carry on the subway back to the hotel!

New York City was very cold and windy, and we did a lot of walking. It was difficult with all the people and the up-and-down sidewalks and steps to the subway. Emily is a trouper and kept up pretty well but was, once again, very tired at the end of the day.

January 4 … John, the girls, and I went to Times Square Church, and it was very special. The choir was inspiring and the service was uplifting. People had to stand in line to get a seat!

We went to the matinee performance of *The Lion King*, with seats front and center. The lights came down, the music started, and as the actors started coming out, I thought to myself, "O dear God, how on Earth can I explain this all to Emily?" As I did, and as she heard the music and all the songs she had loved as a little girl, her face shone with excitement, and the smile she had went from ear to ear!

We had been told to stay in our seats after the show ended. One of the stage managers came over to us and asked Emily if she would like a tour backstage. "Of course!" was the reply!

She got to touch some of the costumes and meet a couple of the actors, including the one who played Zazu. She even got to feel how the bird moved. She was delighted with every aspect of the show, and I felt so honored to be a part of it.

January 5, 6, 7 … The girls and I walked several blocks to Tiffany's. My sister-in-law had suggested that Emily look for a gift from there as a memory. She ended up getting a very sweet bracelet (that was affordable!), and loved it when Sarah and I described the beautiful box and gift bag! We all went to the Empire State Building, had some special macaroni and cheese, shopped in Chinatown, and took the ferry to the Statue of Liberty and Ellis Island.

We returned home, all of us full of memories of a wonderful trip. I know in my heart that the chance is great that this will be the last vacation that all of us will take together.

CHAPTER 18

January 8 … Reality always slams me in the face when I return home from vacation! I had a meeting in school with all of Emily's teachers, as well as the aides who will be helping her. Most of them have never worked with a blind student before, but all are eager for the challenge. They are happy she is returning to school and want to do whatever they can to help her ease back into the routine. I feel like Emily is just accepting the inevitable (having to go to school), instead of embracing it.

January 20 … Emily's first day back in school went well, at least concerning her health. The emotional and relational aspect—not so well. All the friends she had made as a freshman seemed to have moved on without her; other than a couple saying "hi," they didn't interact with her at all.

I knew that today would be the most difficult, and having it behind us will be great. Each day should get better. She will go for the first three periods and get picked up at 10:50 a.m. She rides to school with a friend and neighbor, who also did her homebound teaching.

January 23 ... I told Emily that I had gotten my hair cut and I now have bangs. I asked her if she could picture me that way and she replied, "Yes, but I remember you the way you looked the last time I saw you." Then she added, "I wonder if that's how it will be even when you get old?" It made me think I sure hope I had looked good on the morning of September 2, since that's how she will remember me!

January 24 ... Emily and I went to the dentist this morning. There was an older man also waiting in the lobby. I took Emily in first for her cleaning, and when I came back to sit down, the man spoke to me. He asked if she was blind and I said, "Yes, she lost her sight about five months ago." He said that in observing her for the few moments that he did, she touched his heart and he would pray for her. He continued, "A person has to be careful how they pray because God hears every prayer."

It reminded me of the prayer that she had prayed before she started high school, about impacting it for Christ. What he said, and the spirit in which he said it, almost made me wonder if I had been in the presence of an angel who had been sent to encourage me.

January 30 ... I worked packing up my store this week and am officially done and unemployed as of today. I have done some internal searching for a transfer opportunity, but nothing has worked out.

I was feeling overwhelmed with everything, and Emily sensed it. She said to me, "Mom, if there's one thing I've learned, it's to trust God. I have to trust Him for everything, and we are going to trust Him about your job, too. It will be okay." Wow! In that moment I was struck with the maturity in those things that are really important. (Note: Thankfully my health insurance would cover us for the next month.)

My 5-year-old niece was playing dominoes with Emily. Emily used to love babysitting for her. Lily said to her, "I'm sorry you can't see," to which Emily replied, "That's okay, I'm just happy to be alive." I'm sure the significance wasn't fully received, but I thought it was profound. Emily doesn't talk a lot about how she is feeling, but many times those feelings come out in her words and actions. There is a supernatural peace about her that is almost contagious.

February 8 ... Isaiah 9:2 says, "The people who walk in darkness WILL SEE a great light." I'm claiming that for Emily, but really, it is for each one of us.

We had a guest speaker in church this morning. She was about 15 minutes into her sermon when Emily leaned over to me and said she didn't feel well. Her stomach hurt, she was hot, and she felt dizzy. I asked her if she thought she could walk out. (We always sit in the front row of church.) She said she didn't think she could. So John and I walked her out between us.

John stayed with her and I got the car. While I was pulling up, she fainted. John carried her out and put her in the car. I called the pediatrician's office in town, as we would go to the closest hospital. We were almost there when the on-call doctor called. I explained what was going on and Emily's history. He said, "Well, you're at the hospital now, and they can figure out what's wrong." Several hours later—after a blood test, a urine test, and x-rays—they still had no clue why she had fainted and, because she felt better by this time, they discharged her. This is certainly one episode I don't hope to repeat anytime soon!

February 23 ... Sarah has wanted a dog for as long as I can remember, but we have always said it wasn't the right time. (And I didn't want to end up doing all the work that goes with a dog!) I knew that she understood all the time and focus that was spent on Emily, but I still felt she wasn't getting the attention she needed. So, after much research to find a non-shedding dog, she and John drove to an Atlanta pound and found a Cairn terrier, which we named Woody. Sarah was thrilled. We've hoped that Emily would warm up to having a dog, but that hasn't happened.

March 16 ... The MRI today showed no change in the tumor. The doctors are pleased that it hasn't grown and that it shows signs of "stability." It's hard to be encouraged when we were believing for it to be gone or to be smaller.

Emily has settled into the routine of school. She is tired most days and is certainly never eager to go, but she knows she has to. Her peers still are distant to her, but the adults in her life continue to be amazed by her attitude. We are on a first-name basis with the pharmacist and the technicians at the pharmacy where we get Emily's medications.

Sarah got her learner's permit, and Emily has mentioned how hard it is knowing that she will never drive. She keeps so many of her emotions bottled up inside of her that I didn't think how painful it might be for her younger sister to be able to drive when she never will.

March 24 … I have had a terrible sore throat for several days and didn't want to go to the doctor because we didn't have any insurance. I finally went, was diagnosed with strep throat, and had a bill for $125! Feeling so badly already, I was near tears. Emily sensed it and said, "Mom, I don't understand a lot of things, and I ask God questions and get no answers. What I do know is that it's better to accept things and move on, than to be bitter and resentful."

April 27 … Severe budget cuts in our state have caused some tenured teachers to not be offered contracts for the upcoming school year. The teacher that Emily has been so close to is one of those not coming back to her school. She has been an amazing source of encouragement and has taken time to teach Emily a very visual subject—math—in a very hands-on and oral way.

Emily isn't handling her teacher's leaving well at all. The other teacher with whom she has been close has accepted an administrative position with another school district. I have done my best to tell her that there are other teachers who will step to the plate and need to be touched by her life.

May 23 … In church this morning, there was a time when people could receive prayer from one of the prayer teams. Emily asked to go forward. When we got to the couple who would pray with us, Emily said, "Please just agree with me for my miracle. I don't want to let it slip from my heart and mind."

The newspaper photographer/reporter we had met at the Christmas assembly came to our house in January and interviewed and photographed Emily. She wrote a story about her, headlined "Believing Without Seeing." It was a great article, testifying to the goodness of God in spite of what we see—or in this case, don't see.

June 23 … We traveled to Denver, Colorado, for a pastors conference and spent some time afterward in the mountains with dear friends. It was a great time of relaxing and was refreshing for all of us.

One afternoon, Emily went shopping with a couple of the girls and their mom. When she got back, my friend started crying and said, "What an honor to be her guide for the afternoon." She said Emily was so cheerful and easygoing, that she was a delight to be with.

July 10 … Emily is at a camp for visually impaired kids at Hilton Head Island for the week. She's had a blast—she's played putt-putt, gone shark fishing, kayaking, and swimming in the Atlantic. It's been great for her to do things that she didn't know she could do. It's also been wonderful for her to meet peers who have an understanding of what she deals with on a daily basis.

July 23 … Matthew, Emily, and I drove to Durham, North Carolina, to Duke University Children's Hospital. I have been so frustrated that no one has been able to figure out Emily's chronic headaches. I made an appointment to see a headache specialist in the pediatric neurology department, and because we were going so far, I also made appointments with a pediatric endocrinologist and pediatric ophthalmologist.

Our first appointment was with the headache specialist. Emily and I both liked her right away. We were with her for over an hour, and she was confident that we can find relief from the headaches. She couldn't see any underlying issue causing them, and said she would bring Emily's case before a panel of physicians to get their opinions.

July 24 … We spent the night and saw the ophthalmologist first thing in the morning. Her diagnosis was the same— permanent vision loss. However, she was more positive that medical advancements could be made in Emily's lifetime that could enable her to see again.

The endocrinologist was encouraging as well. She concurred with the plan our endocrinologist has. Then she said that many of her patients who have had craniopharyngioma resections end up being obese because they can't control their sense of feeling full. Even though I talked with her about Emily's weight gain and puffiness, she said Emily looks great and to not worry. Overall, I am really glad we went.

August 16 … Most parents remember their child's first day of school. I relived that today as Emily left for her first full day of school in 1½ years.

When they leave for kindergarten, you know the world will be theirs, and you wonder as a mother if you have done everything you could to prepare them for the journey. As I watched her leave, I couldn't control my emotions as I wondered how she will make it, not just at school today, but the rest of her life.

Ephesians 3:20 says, "He is able to do exceedingly and abundantly above all we can ask or think." And Psalm 30:11 says, "Thou hast turned my mourning into dancing … that my soul may sing praise to Thee and not be silent. O Lord, my God, I will give thanks to Thee forever."

FAMILY POETRY

Move from the Pages (1)
By John Zimmermann

The God of the Bible moves from the pages,

And takes my hand as the battle rages.

I'm Abraham, Isaac, and Jacob's God, but I am also yours, why think it odd?

"I'll never leave, I'll never go," Yes, Dear Jesus, now I know,

These words You mean, for even me, though almost blind, I know she'll see.

When I am strong and full of fight, feeling faith's increasing might,

You're there encouraging, cheering on, leading till the battle's won.

When I am weak and full of sin, knowing my faults from deep within,

You call "come," You don't hide Your face, You offer Your amazing grace.

There are people and places that I recall, some are vivid, they are memories all.

But through life's journeys ups and downs, there's too much joy to wear a frown.

To know my life is lived with You, intertwined like grass and dew,

Is even as the Psalmist penned, far too wondrous to comprehend?

Emily (2)
By LP Zimmermann

Emily

Gently

I'll cradle you

With my tears

All will be well

And

You will

Have no fears.

The Lord above

Has us covered

In a blanket

Of love

That is

Always

Near.

I think

Of you often,

As you are

So dear

To my heart

And my art.

The messages sent

Are received

With great joy.

Your Aunt Resa

Knows a thing

About this.

Contact her now

And ask her how she

Dealt with emotions

Flowing from

This seeming abyss.

Epilogue

Emily graduated from high school in June 2010 in the top 10 percent of her class. Ten days after graduating, she flew by herself to Littleton, Colorado, to attend an Independence Training Program for blind and visually impaired students. She was taught life skills as well as technology, Braille, and travel.

She loved the weather and especially the public transportation in Denver, so she applied to and was accepted at Metropolitan State University of Denver. At the time of this writing, she is a senior and looking forward to graduating in the spring of 2017 with a major in speech communications and a minor in English.

Emily has had numerous opportunities to share her story to varied assemblies. She has spoken to private and public high schools, church youth groups, professional organizations and special education educators and families. She loves to encourage her audiences to not give up, no matter what they are going through. Hers is a story of determination, perseverance and faith.

Her contact information is brokencrayonsejz.com and her email address is brokencrayonsejz@gmail.com. If you want to hear a story of courage and hope, please reach out to her.

Someone asked Emily how she can deal with this on a daily basis, and this is what she said: "I could be angry and frustrated with my life, and bitter at God, but I would still be blind. How much better to have a positive attitude and a thankful and grateful spirit, because I will still be blind."

Emily has tried more prescription medicines than can be counted to relieve her headaches, but so far each has been unsuccessful. She is plagued with a headache every day of her life. We remain hopeful that one day she will be not only headache-free, but tumor-free as well, as a small piece still remains. She has tried many other non-medical, homeopathic treatments, too.

Emily has an infectious laugh and is a joy and delight to everyone around her. She continues to have a positive attitude about her situation and is eager to move on in her life. While in high school it was difficult to find acceptance from her peers, she feels that now that she is beyond that time—that new doors of opportunity, as well as new friendships, will open up to her.

Our prayer is for the light of Jesus to shine through her, so that is what people see, instead of her physical eyes that don't see. There isn't a day that goes by that isn't a struggle for her.

It is so difficult as her Mom to see the pain and the difficulty and to not be able to do anything about it. I see the people stare at her and want to say, "Haven't you ever seen a white cane, or a person that is visually impaired?" Whether it is in ignorance or curiosity, it still hurts.

Today I am more confident than ever that God has a plan for Emily's life. While the life I see her living isn't what I would have chosen for her, I know that He will use Emily's story to impact lives ... one at a time.

ABOUT THE AUTHOR

Janet is a first-time author. Born and raised in Minnesota, she moved with her husband, John, to South Carolina to raise their four children. John has been a pastor for 25 years. She is now living in Colorado and making the most of life in the beautiful landscape of the Rocky Mountains.

Made in the USA
Lexington, KY
15 May 2017